For John, Thomas and
Emma,
Maybe someday you too
will swim with sharks!

Lisa Cook

Enjoy the book!
Joel Simonetti

Why I Care About
SHARKS

Will Sharks Survive This Century?

Lisa Cook and **Joel Simonetti**

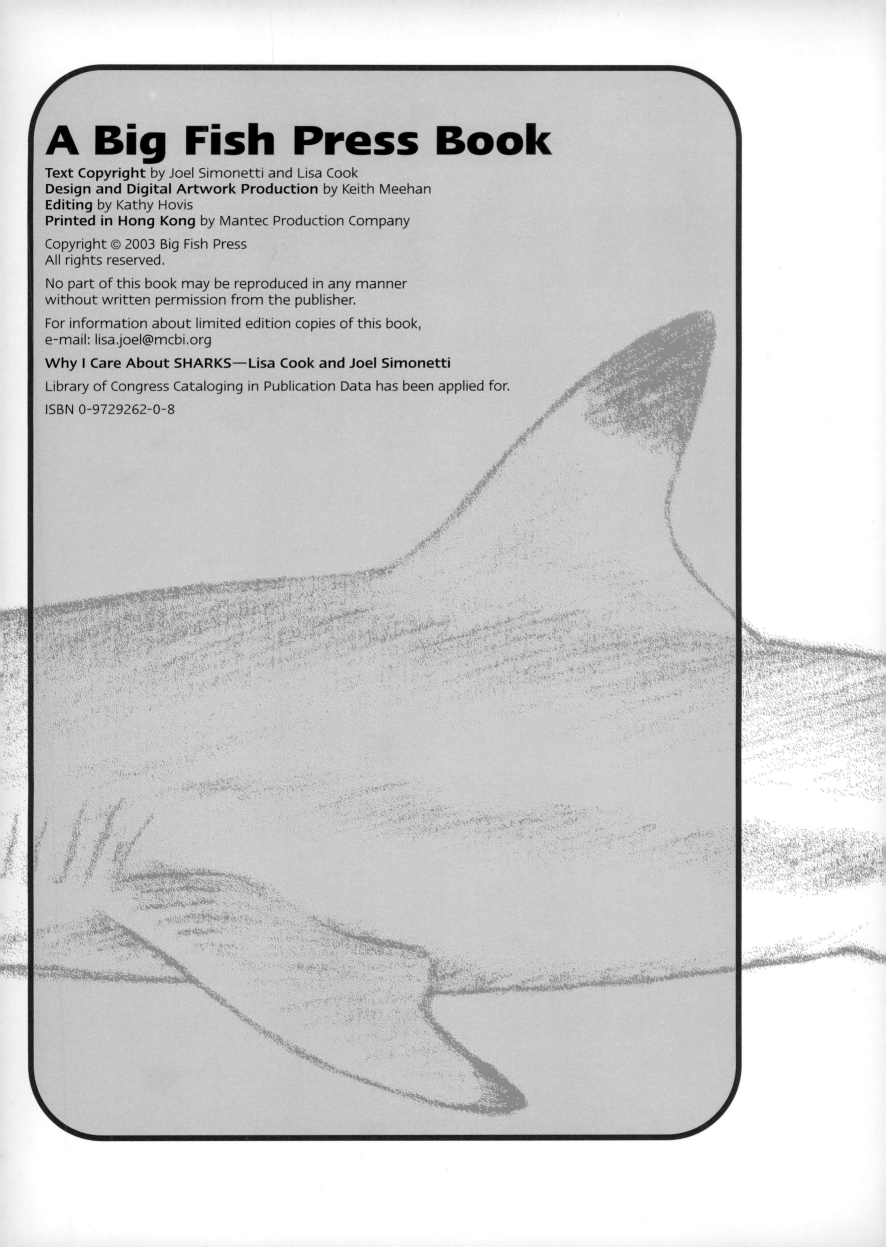

A Big Fish Press Book

Text Copyright by Joel Simonetti and Lisa Cook
Design and Digital Artwork Production by Keith Meehan
Editing by Kathy Hovis
Printed in Hong Kong by Mantec Production Company

For information about limited edition copies of this book,
e-mail: lisa.joel@mcbi.org

Why I Care About SHARKS—Lisa Cook and Joel Simonetti

Library of Congress Cataloging in Publication Data has been applied for.
ISBN 0-9729262-0-8

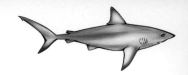

Dedications

To my mom who bought me a butterfly net, and to my dad who gave me my first fishing rod. —J.S.

To my children who generously and patiently teach me . . . Justice about compassion and wisdom, Sahana about courage and tenacity, and Finn about joy and laughter . . . and to all parents who welcome the chance to learn from their kids. —L.C.

Acknowledgements

We now understand why acknowledgements in many books go on and on. The work of a book belongs to no single person, or in our case, couple. This book would never have been possible without the work of scientists, researchers, and other thinkers whose ideas and discoveries we have drawn upon, or without the contributions and support of dozens of other people. For their can-do attitudes, good advice and unlimited generosity, we thank Dr. Julia Parrish and Tony Wu. For his wit and work editing and educating us about sharks, we owe Dr. John Morrissey a debt of gratitude. The patient editing of Kathy Hovis improved our manuscript in countless ways. Without the boundless creativity and talent of our friend Keith Meehan, this book would never have been possible.

We're also grateful to Dr. Elliott Norse, Katie Burdick, Dr. Lance Morgan and Tina Harcrow for opening their door and giving us a home at the Marine Conservation Biology Institute. To Victor Wu, Becky Zug, Elizabeth Murdock, Steve Trent and Peter Knights of WildAid, thanks for the use of your photographs and for your enormous concern on behalf of sharks and people.

Dr. Ian Dutton, Dr. Mark Erdmann and Dr. Carl Safina inspired us and gave us crucial, initial support. Dr. Bernd Cordes gave us a chance and continues to help us. Other people to whom we're grateful include: Dr. Merry Camhi, John Davis, Kate Litle, Dr. Shelley Clarke, Dr. Lida Pet-Soede, Rachel Cavanagh, Roxanne Meehan, Sue Dabritz-Yuen, Evelyn Cook, and Bob, Jeff and Joyce Cannon.

A huge thanks also goes out to all the photographers who have dedicated their lives to understanding and documenting the beauty of our oceans and the tragedy of their abuse and neglect. This book could not have been made without their generous contribution of discounted, and in many instances, free photos. To the book's illustrators, Kate Spencer and Rod Bambao, thank you for putting your hearts into this work.

We also want to thank Dr. Jim Jarvie and Laurie Pierce for opening our eyes to other possibilities. And to our "dushis" Alix, Bob, Darryl and Jerry, thanks for jumping off all of those Curaçao cliffs with us in pursuit of sharks.

Finally, we'd like to remember Dr. Bob Johannes. May we always follow your example—believing in the ideas of others and in people's ability to learn from the past and mold a better future.

Despite all of the assistance that we have received, we bear responsibility for any errors, of judgment or fact, contained within this book. —J.S. & L.C.

Contents

How Much is Enough?

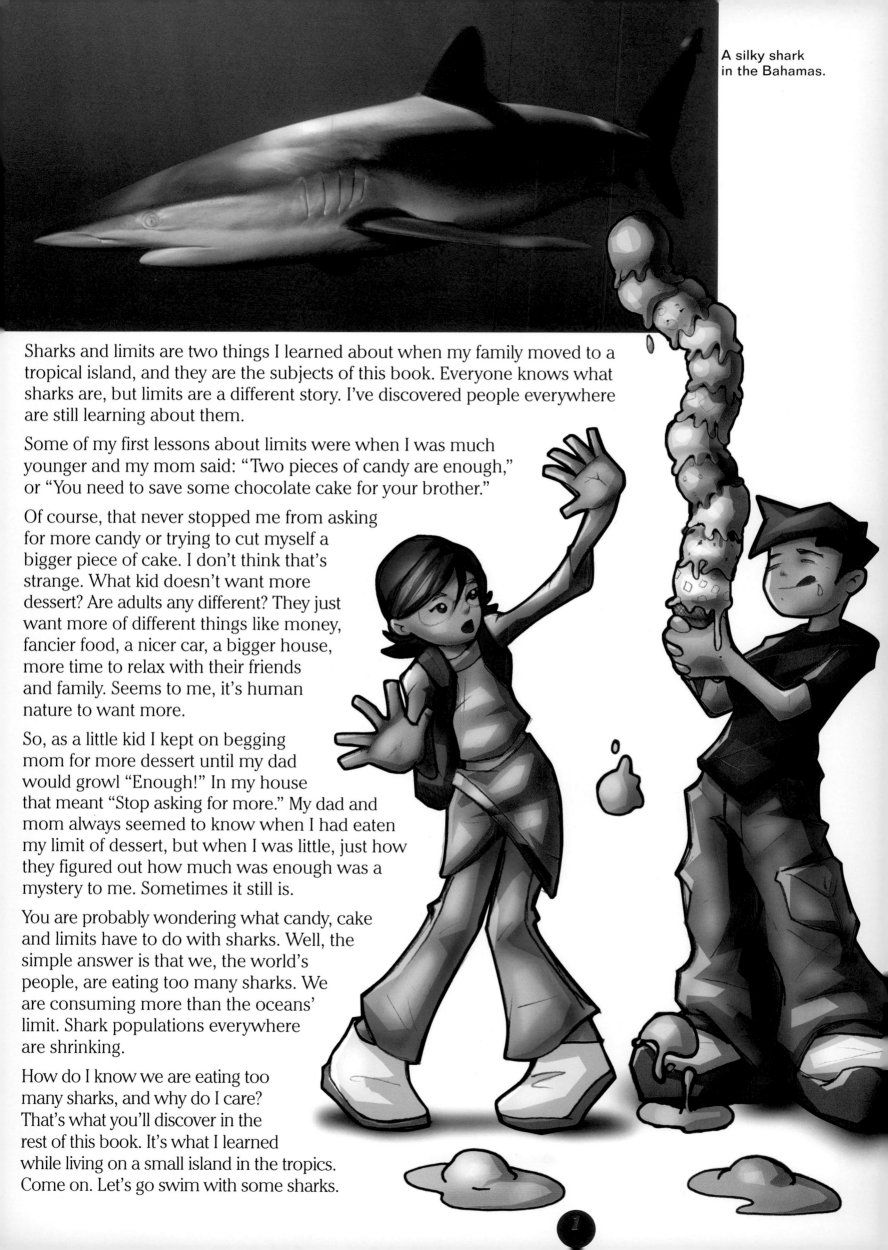

A silky shark in the Bahamas.

Sharks and limits are two things I learned about when my family moved to a tropical island, and they are the subjects of this book. Everyone knows what sharks are, but limits are a different story. I've discovered people everywhere are still learning about them.

Some of my first lessons about limits were when I was much younger and my mom said: "Two pieces of candy are enough," or "You need to save some chocolate cake for your brother."

Of course, that never stopped me from asking for more candy or trying to cut myself a bigger piece of cake. I don't think that's strange. What kid doesn't want more dessert? Are adults any different? They just want more of different things like money, fancier food, a nicer car, a bigger house, more time to relax with their friends and family. Seems to me, it's human nature to want more.

So, as a little kid I kept on begging mom for more dessert until my dad would growl "Enough!" In my house that meant "Stop asking for more." My dad and mom always seemed to know when I had eaten my limit of dessert, but when I was little, just how they figured out how much was enough was a mystery to me. Sometimes it still is.

You are probably wondering what candy, cake and limits have to do with sharks. Well, the simple answer is that we, the world's people, are eating too many sharks. We are consuming more than the oceans' limit. Shark populations everywhere are shrinking.

How do I know we are eating too many sharks, and why do I care? That's what you'll discover in the rest of this book. It's what I learned while living on a small island in the tropics. Come on. Let's go swim with some sharks.

First

Recalling the first shark I ever saw is like remembering a dream. It was three years ago, and I was 13. That day my friend Jackie and I went snorkeling at a place we'd never been. It was off a remote part of our island where there are no roads, at the end of a point of land that sticks out into the sea. You have to climb over a lot of rocks to get there and usually the water off the point is too rough to swim in, but on this day, it was calm.

I met Jackie shortly after my family moved to the island. We had a lot in common. Some kids were into collecting game cards, music, and playing video and computer games, but not Jackie and me. What we thought was cool was snorkeling and SCUBA diving over the coral reefs that surrounded our island. To swim with sharks was our ultimate dream. Between us we owned 27 books about sea life. We searched through every magazine looking for articles about the oceans. We surfed the Internet for even more information. I had a collection of pictures of sea creatures that I had downloaded off the Internet. I had them organized in folders. Whales in one. Sharks in another. Reef fish, sea turtles, and so on. Weekends and after school, Jackie and I tried to identify everything we saw snorkeling and diving. My mother said we were obsessed, but we couldn't help ourselves. Everything underwater was so new and beautiful.

Our island is surrounded by a coral reef, one that grows close to shore, just beyond the beach. It's a great reef for kids. We don't need a boat to get to it. The morning I saw my first shark, we hid our bikes in some bushes where the road ended, and, as the sun rose, we hiked a long way to the point. As we kicked away from shore, swimming side by side, the water felt cool, but our heads were boiling with thoughts. "What's down there? What are we going to see?"

A grey reef shark in the Pacific Ocean's Marshall Islands.

Encounter

That day, when Jackie and I first swam off the point, we felt like Lucy in *The Lion the Witch and the Wardrobe*. It was as if we had found a secret passage into a fantastic and mysterious new world. Beneath us an entire hillside of soft corals and sea fans waved back and forth. The place was alive with fish–some we'd never seen–swirling around like thousands of leaves caught in a breeze. Suddenly a sea turtle glided beneath us like a bird riding the wind on a hot, lazy day. Jackie dove, leaving a trail of silvery bubbles as she kicked toward the turtle for a closer look. I watched her grow smaller and smaller before I lifted my flippers over my head and kicked down to join her. Then, for some reason, I stopped a few meters below the surface. Hanging there I turned and looked out toward the deeper water into the face of a shark swimming right toward me!

A lifetime of movies and TV shows had prepared me to fear for my life. It would sure be dramatic if I could say I reached for a knife strapped to my leg and used some kick-boxing moves to drive the shark away. But the truth is, I just froze, mesmerized by the way the shark swam. It reminded me of a horse running in slow motion. I could see all its body parts and muscles flexing and working together. It seemed so graceful and confident, like an Olympic runner who knows he's going to win the race, and raises his arms in victory.

Was I scared? Sure, but mostly I was in awe. Before I realized what had happened the shark turned and swam past me. I stared after it, and even took a few kicks to follow as it disappeared into the blue. Today, when I think about seeing that shark, it's like a dream. I worry one day I'll wake up, and I won't be able to remember how I felt. Seeing that shark filled me with a sense of wonder and freedom. I only wish it hadn't swum away so soon.

Food for Thought

"A man should not be ashamed of coarse food, humble clothing, and modest dwelling, but should only be ashamed in not being cultivated in the perception of beauty."
—Young-hill Kang

Resistance

Ever stuck your arm out of the window of a fast-moving car and held your hand up vertically, palm against the wind? The air pushes hard against your hand making it tough to hold in place. When wind or water pushes against something, we call it **resistance**. What if you lay your palm down horizontally? Is it easier to keep your arm in place? This is because there's less resistance. The easier an object can move, the faster it can go.

When you held your hand flat, you made it **aerodynamic**. Its shape created little **resistance** or **drag**. Sometimes you hear the word **hydrodynamic**. This refers to ease of movement in the water. Fast boats, cars, planes and fish have similar, low resistance shapes.

The snout of a fast shark, like the front of a fast car, is shaped like a flattened cone. With no large, flat surface for air or water to push against, it slips easily through the water.

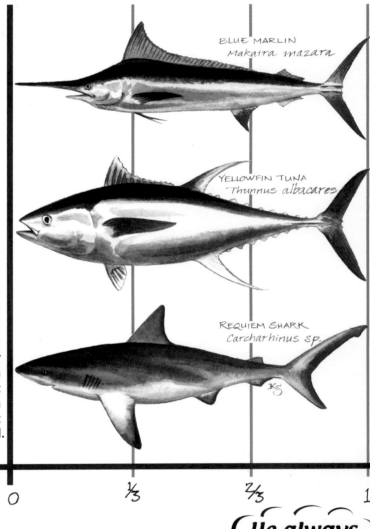

BLUE MARLIN
Makaira mazara

YELLOWFIN TUNA
Thunnus albacares

REQUIEM SHARK
Carcharhinus sp.

0   1/3   2/3   1

Built for Speed

Experiments have shown that the most hydrodynamic body shape, one shared by fast fish and fast boats, is one in which the front 1/3 swells up from the snout to its thickest point and then the rear 2/3 tapers away. The fastest ocean predators, like tunas, dolphins, sharks and billfish are built this way. We often refer to this shape as being **streamlined**.

FAST CARS!

He always forgets about fast fish

OUR OCEANS

Fast Fish

What kind of shark had I seen? At home, I checked all my books and pictures. At school, I took everything out of the library. I even looked on the Internet, but I still couldn't tell. I discovered there are about 500 species of sharks, and many seen near coral reefs look similar. The marine biologist at the local aquarium asked me some tough questions.

"Did your shark have one or two large dorsal fins?"

"Dorsal fins?"

"The ones on top," he explained.

"I don't know. I didn't notice."

"Was the mouth of the shark you saw at the very front of its head or was it underneath its snout?" he asked.

"Underneath."

"OK, we know you didn't see a whale shark," he said. "Was its mouth only on the bottom of its head, or did it wrap around the side of its snout?"

"It wrapped around."

"OK, you didn't see a shark that lives on the bottom, like a nurse shark."

Swimming fast is not important for sharks that live on the bottom. This angel shark looks like it's been squashed, but its flat shape helps it camouflage and bury itself in the sand, so it can ambush its prey.

Our conversation went like that. Mostly he helped me figure out what I didn't see. I didn't see any of the big plankton-eating sharks such as a whale shark, basking shark or a megamouth. I didn't see a hammerhead, a great white, or a tiger shark, which has a distinctive pattern of bars on its body. Neither was it a blacktip shark or one of the several kinds of whitetip sharks. The tips of the fins of the shark I saw were the same grey color as its body. It wasn't a thresher, a shark with a tail as long as its body.

It could have been a sharpnosed shark, a milk shark, a lemon shark, a galapagos shark, a bull shark, one of the reef sharks, or . . . you get the picture. I didn't notice enough about the shark to identify it. It could have been one of many that share a body shape that makes them some of the sea's fastest fish.

A blue shark shows its speedy, streamlined shape.

Food for Thought
Swimming Speeds

bluefin tuna – 80 kph

sailfish – 75 kph

orca (killer whale) – 55.2 kph

shortfin mako shark – 49.6 kph

blue whale – 47.6 kph

blue shark – 39.2 kph

dolphin – 37.8 kph

human – 8.1 kph

eel – 3.8 kph

Speeds are estimates because fish are difficult to clock as they don't swim in straight lines.

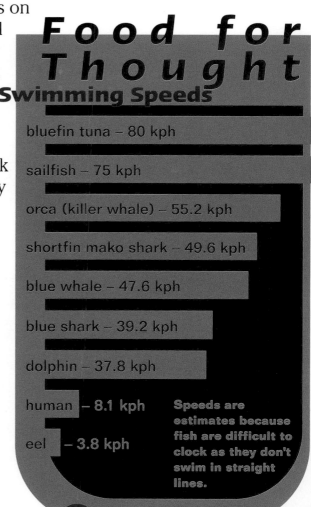

great white shark: Hot

swordfish: **Hotter**

Hot

bluefin tuna: **Hottest**

Hot Fish

Scientists have discovered that a few big fish, including some sharks, tuna and billfish (like swordfish and marlin) can keep at least parts of their bodies warm. In this way they are more like birds and mammals than reptiles. These "hot fish" recycle the heat produced by their muscles, using it to warm up their blood after it passes through their gills.

How do they do it? In these hot fish, blood vessels are compacted closely together in the middle of their bodies letting cold blood, coming from the gills, flow right next to the warm blood leaving their muscles. This heats up the cold blood before delivering it to the fish's swimming muscles, eyes, brain and other organs. This unique heat exchange system gives these huge, hot fish an edge over their cold-bodied prey.

Cold

Sharks don't need to open their mouths nearly this much to breathe, but with its jaws wide open, you can see how water flows into a shark's mouth and out through its gills.

Cold Bodies

Most fish are the same temperature as the water. Those in polar regions are colder than those that live close to the equator. This is because of the way fish breathe. Small blood vessels in the gills absorb oxygen from the water and carry it throughout the shark's body. Because these blood vessels come in contact with the cold water flowing through the gills, the blood in them is quickly chilled.

When all the oxygen in the blood has been used up, vessels carry the blood back to the gills to pick up more. At this time, the blood is warmer because it has been inside the fish's body close to its warm muscles, but that heat is lost as soon as it flows back through the cold gills.

Hot Fish

A year after I saw my first shark, I saw another diving with my shark-crazy uncle in much colder waters off New Zealand, an island nation east of Australia. This time there was no mistaking what kind it was. Its nose was a perfect cone and when it swam by, its teeth were visible. But what really helped me identify it was its crescent-moon tail–the top-half nearly a mirror image of the bottom. This shark was swift enough to hunt the ocean's greatest athletes—fish like swordfish and marlin and mammals like dolphins and porpoises. I had seen the fastest shark of all, a mako.

It swam in from deep water and passed the edge of a steep drop-off where my uncle and I were watching a school of big silver fish. What makes a mako fast is not just its aerodynamic shape and powerful tail, but also its body heat. I read that mako sharks are one of only a few of the world's roughly 27,000 species of fish that have warm bodies. This is a great advantage. A warm animal can swim faster, see better and think and react more quickly than one that's cold.

Most fish are cold-bodied like reptiles. Consider Komodo dragons—the fierce ambush hunters that live on a few islands in eastern Indonesia. The world's largest lizards, Komodos can grow to more than 3 meters and weigh 250 kilograms. In some ways they're like certain sharks. Their teeth are serrated, and they surprise their prey, biting out a large chunk of a water buffalo or deer and then waiting for it to bleed to death. But on cool mornings, Komodos are about as dangerous as geckos. Because they are cold-bodied, they have to bask in the sun to warm up their muscles before they can go hunting.

Makos, and other hot fish, don't need the sun to get warm. Built into their bodies is a system that lets them reuse the heat their swimming muscles produce to warm their eyes and brain and even help them digest their food faster.

Food for Thought

When mammals exercise, they breathe heavily and get hot quickly. You might think exercise would warm up a fish too, but it doesn't. When a fish is swimming, it does breathe more heavily (just like us), but all this does is move its blood more quickly through its gills cooling it down even faster.

A mako shark, the fastest shark in the sea.

Warm Bodies

Most mammals and birds can keep their bodies warm all of the time because they eat a lot more food than reptiles and fish. More than 80% of the food warm-bodied animals eat is used to keep them warm. Birds and mammals also have layers of fat and fur or feathers that keep heat in. It's a great advantage. Being warm, they can hunt anytime, even in the snow and at night.

Smell

Sharks have a keen sense of smell. Unlike humans, who use their nostrils for breathing and smelling, sharks use their nostrils, or **nares**, only for detecting scents. A shark's nares are located on the front of its snout and are about 10,000 times more powerful than our nostrils. Just one drop of liquid tuna fish in a large swimming pool is enough to give a shark a whiff of dinner.

Sight

Some people think sharks are blind but most have fantastic eyesight. Some can see in color, and the ones that hunt at night can see as well as nocturnal predators like cats. What gives people the impression that sharks are blind? There are several things.

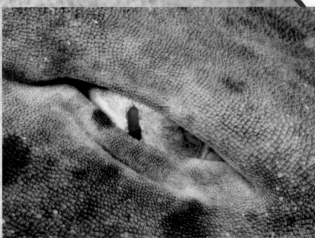

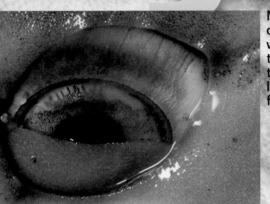

Many sharks have an extra eyelid called a **nictitating membrane**, which closes when they attack their prey. This membrane protects the eye and gives it a shiny, glassy look, which many people mistake for blindness.

A shark's eyes can also look blind when they are at the surface of the water because the sun is so bright there. This causes their pupils to constrict (become tiny) so much that they are barely visible.

Other sharks roll their eyes back in their heads when they attack. This makes their eyes look like white marbles, but keeps them from being scratched or poked by prey. Here a great white lunging for some bait has rolled its eye back to protect it.

Taste

Sharks sometimes nibble fish and spit them out if they don't like their taste. Some experts believe many shark attacks are actually sharks just trying to find out whether people are something good to eat. Since we are not the favorite food of sharks, after a taste they usually swim away.

Touch

Although they don't have fingers, sharks do have a sense of touch. Sharks have been seen feeling other animals with their snouts. Nurse sharks have whiskers, called **barbels**, (which you can see in the photo with the diver on the next page) hanging near their nares and mouth. They use their barbels to feel around in the sand for food.

Shark Sense

Smell
Sight
Taste
Touch

When I was 12, a year before I saw my fist shark, I took my first dive, but I was so frightened, I almost didn't go. I remember sitting on the side of the boat in the sun with my gear on. I was wearing a mask, flippers, weights, a heavy SCUBA tank and a black wetsuit that made me so hot I felt like I was wearing a plastic garbage bag. Over the edge of the boat I could see coral and lots of beautiful fish below, but I just couldn't make myself get in the water.

Finally seasickness pushed me overboard. The waves were lifting and dropping our small boat making my stomach rise and fall like it was on a roller coaster. I couldn't wait any longer. If I didn't get in, I was going to be sick. I looked at my dad, who was sitting across from me in his own black wetsuit, for some encouragement. With his nose crinkled and his mouth molded into a scowl, he looked like he'd just sniffed my baby brother's diaper. "What are you waiting for?" he said. "Let's go!"

I was going to get no help from Dad, but I could tell he was nervous and probably as scared and seasick as I was. What were we afraid of? Sharks, of course. We'd heard that with their amazing senses they could detect a diver more than a kilometer away. And, I knew what would happen if a shark sensed me . . . . At least that's what I thought when I was 12.

A diver with nurse sharks in Thailand.

Food for Thought

"We need another and a wiser and a more mystical concept of animals . . . . We patronize them for their incompleteness, for their tragic fate at having taken form so far below ourselves. And therein we err, and greatly err. For the animal shall not be measured by man. In a world . . . more complete than ours they move finished . . . , gifted with extensions of the senses we have lost or never attained, living by voices we shall never hear." — Henry Beston, The Outermost House

Pit Organs

Sharks have slight depressions in their skin on their heads and back called **pit organs**. Shark scientists disagree about their function. Some think they're extra tasting organs. Others believe they tell sharks how deep they are swimming. Still, others suspect they give sharks information about the salt content of the water.

A bronze whaler shark in Australian waters.

Vibrations

Hearing and Distant Touch

Why do sharks seem to magically appear when a fish is struggling on a fisherman's line? In the water, moving objects create ripples or vibrations like the circles you see when you throw a rock into a pond. Swimming fish create patterns of vibrations, which change when a fish is injured or struggling. Sharks sense the difference because they can hear and feel vibrations.

Although you can't see them, a shark has ears with openings connected to tiny tubes at the top of its skull. Sound vibrations travel into these tubes and down to the shark's inner ear where a shark hears sounds that come from far away. The inner ear also tells a shark which way is up, similar to our inner ear, which gives us information about balance.

Another organ called the **lateral line** helps a shark detect closer vibrations. The lateral line runs from the head to the tail on both sides of a shark's body. Lateral lines feel patterns of vibrations and sense when they change. Many people call this sense "distant touch." So, a shark can actually hear and feel a fish struggling on a line long before it sees it.

Electrical Impulses

Hammerheads have more ampullae of Lorenzini than any other shark species.

A Sixth Sense

Like a metal detector that can locate buried pirate treasure, a shark has the ability to find prey buried in the sand or hidden in reef caves and crevices. They do this by sensing the electricity all animals naturally produce. Sharks sense these electrical impulses in special jelly filled canals called the **ampullae of Lorenzini**. (Lorenzini was the scientist who discovered them.) Look closely at the picture of the hammerhead's snout (on the left) and you can see the tiny openings to these canals.

Using this sense, sharks find creatures like sting rays and fish that bury themselves in sand. Unfortunately for these fish, their bodies' electrical fields reveal their hiding places. The ampullae of Lorenzini also enable sharks to "see" when their eyes are rolled back in their heads during an attack.

Extra Sense

When Jackie and I began our quest to swim with some sharks, we started carrying wooden clubs to protect ourselves if it were necessary. We did it because although neither of us had yet seen a shark, we knew how good their senses are. Underwater we always felt like we were being watched.

Off the coast of our island, only one person had ever been attacked by a shark, but that didn't make us feel any safer. If it had happened once, we figured . . . . Despite our fear, the story of the shark attack made us laugh. No matter how many old timers we asked, we could never figure out the truth. Half the people told us the man, who was bitten on the leg by the shark and survived, was in the water cleaning his boat. The rest told us he was in the water butchering a goat. People did eat a lot of goat meat on our island.

We got our wooden clubs, "shark billies" we called them, at the hardware store. Jackie had seen a television show in which the divers starring in the program had said that shark billies were all a diver needed to fight off an aggressive shark. It sounded good to us, but since there was no "billy" section at the hardware store, we bought broom handles instead. It wasn't easy swimming underwater with a 150-centimeter broomstick. Eventually, I cut mine in half.

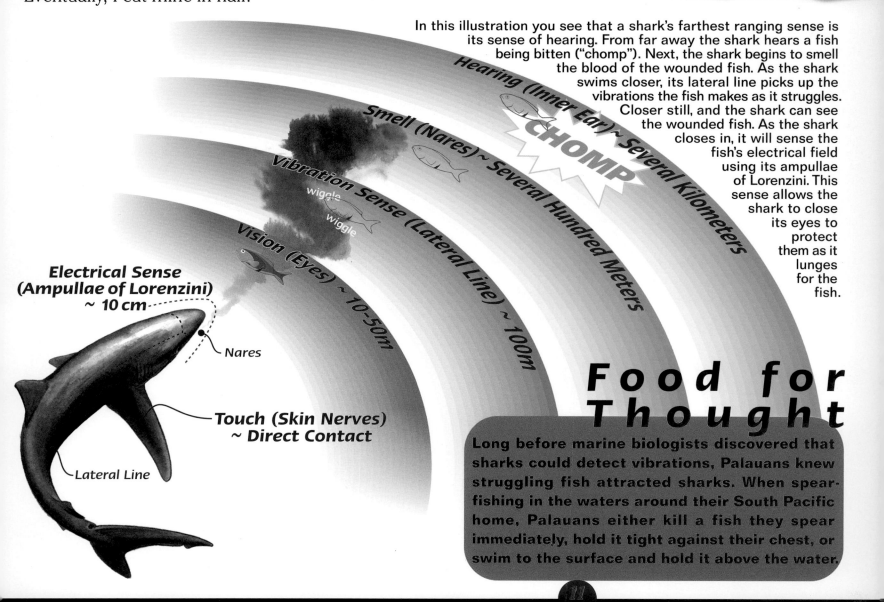

In this illustration you see that a shark's farthest ranging sense is its sense of hearing. From far away the shark hears a fish being bitten ("chomp"). Next, the shark begins to smell the blood of the wounded fish. As the shark swims closer, its lateral line picks up the vibrations the fish makes as it struggles. Closer still, and the shark can see the wounded fish. As the shark closes in, it will sense the fish's electrical field using its ampullae of Lorenzini. This sense allows the shark to close its eyes to protect them as it lunges for the fish.

Hearing (Inner Ear) ~ Several Kilometers

Smell (Nares) ~ Several Hundred Meters

Vibration Sense (Lateral Line) ~ 100m

Vision (Eyes) ~ 10-50m

CHOMP

wiggle

Wiggle

Electrical Sense (Ampullae of Lorenzini) ~ 10 cm

Nares

Touch (Skin Nerves) ~ Direct Contact

Lateral Line

Food for Thought

Long before marine biologists discovered that sharks could detect vibrations, Palauans knew struggling fish attracted sharks. When spearfishing in the waters around their South Pacific home, Palauans either kill a fish they spear immediately, hold it tight against their chest, or swim to the surface and hold it above the water.

Sharks with Spiracles

Ram Ventilation

Not all sharks can rest on the bottom and breathe. Many species, like these blue sharks, have to swim continuously with their mouths open so water will flow through their gills. This method of breathing is called **ram ventilation**.

A Pumping System

Like a nurse shark, this leopard shark does not need to swim to be able to breathe. Instead it uses a pumping system found in all sharks that rest on the bottom. It opens its mouth, closes its gills, and sucks in a mouthful of water. Then it opens its gills and forces the water through them. Just like the blue shark, the nurse and leopard sharks can also open their mouths and ram ventilate when swimming.

If a Shark Stops Swimming Will it Die?

My billy was the only one that ever touched a shark. It happened one day when Jackie and I were diving over mounds of coral the size of cars in a vast field of seaweed called sargassum. The "coral heads" (Australians call them "bommies") were scattered about like boulders on a grassy lawn. Each one was a little city swarming with fish. We flew like planes from one coral head to another. A big moray eel lived in one. We always stopped in to see him, except on this day.

Instead, we swam past his home, and under a coral head that we'd never before visited we saw a nurse shark. It was about 2 meters long and sleeping with its head hidden in a small cave. Its long tail and body were resting on some sargassum. Jackie and I froze when we spotted the shark and gave each other wide-eyed looks.

As we swam closer, I made sure I counted all the fins and noticed their shape. Finally, we knelt down, so close to the nurse shark that we could see its gill slits opening and closing as it breathed. I remembered my old science textbook having a picture of a shark in it. It said all sharks had to keep moving in order to breathe, and that if they stopped swimming they would die. That's not true. Nurse sharks, and many others, can actually pump water over their gills while they lie on the bottom.

A diver touches a Caribbean reef shark resting on the bottom.

The next thing Jackie did surprised me. She slowly reached out and brushed her fingertips against the nurse shark's tail. The big animal shivered, but that was all. Now feeling even more daring, she gently touched its back and dorsal fins. I couldn't believe it. Excitement was shining out of Jackie's eyes. She grabbed my hand, and the next thing I knew I was touching the nurse shark too. Its skin was like fine sand, smooth and soft. It was gray-green in color and covered with tiny blue and black dots, like those you see when you touch your nose to the television screen and stare.

We stayed there petting the nurse shark until our air ran low, and we had to surface. The last thing I did before we swam up was gently touch a fin of the sleeping shark with my billy. I never brought it diving again.

Food for Thought

The blue shark is a **pelagic** species. This means it lives in the open ocean far from land. Scientists have tagged blue sharks and recorded them swimming all the way across the Pacific Ocean. Unfortunately, each year millions of these high-seas travelers die because they are unable to breathe after they're hooked on lines or entangled in fishing nets. This blue shark suffocated in a Japanese drift net in the North Pacific.

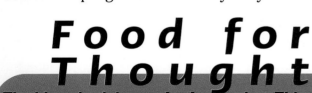

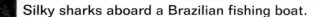
Silky sharks aboard a Brazilian fishing boat.

Keeping Records

Why don't we know precisely how many sharks fishermen kill every year? There are several reasons. Most nations don't require their fishermen to keep a log or diary recording what they catch. Unreliable records are also a problem. To avoid fishing laws or fees on their catches, some fishermen regularly underreport the number of fish they take. Sharks are also frequently caught by mistake and thrown back into the ocean, usually dead. Very few fishermen record the species, or numbers of sharks they catch by accident. This poor record keeping prevents us from learning exactly how many sharks we're killing each year.

Records

Sharks at a market in India.

Empty

Emptying the Piggy Bank

Imagine you have a piggy bank with US$10 in it. Each week your parents also pay you US$1 for jobs you do around the house, and you put your dollar in your piggy bank. Now suppose that each week you also take US$2 dollars out of your piggy bank to buy things. For how many weeks will you be able to keep on taking US$2 spending money out of your bank? How long will your money last?

The oceans are like a giant piggy bank. If fishermen continue catching sharks and other fish faster than they can reproduce, we will eventually empty our oceans?

Some people in the United Arab Emirates think eating juvenile sharks will make them strong.

This hammerhead and the remoras that hitched a ride on it all suffocated after they became entangled in a driftnet in the Arafura Sea between Indonesia and Australia.

How Many Sharks Killed?

Not too long ago, there were a lot more sharks in the waters around our island. I realized this after my dad gave me a book called *Men Beneath the Sea*. It was written by a man named Hans Hass who was one of the first people to SCUBA dive and take pictures underwater. He was also fascinated by sharks. To my surprise, Hass made many of his dives off the island where we were living.

"We were the first to dive on these 'shark infested coasts,'" Hass wrote about our island. "Almost daily we saw large and small specimens; altogether we must have had more than 500 encounters. They (sharks) would come in from the open sea and swim around us especially in the early morning or late afternoon, but usually they kept a respectful distance."

"More than 500 encounters!" I couldn't believe it. Jackie and I had been to the same places as Hass, in waters some people still said were "shark infested," but all we had managed to see were a few shy sharks.

In the 55 years since Hass was here, what happened to all the sharks? Why were there so few compared to his time? I started researching and reading, and what I learned shocked me. We're eating so many sharks today that we're emptying the oceans of them. Most sharks reproduce slowly, and we're killing them faster than they can replace themselves. Our appetite has exceeded the limit of what the seas can sustain.

Scalloped hammerheads like these in Ecuador's Galapagos Islands frequently gather together in large numbers to socialize, find a mate and have their skin cleaned by smaller fish. Twenty years ago divers frequently saw these sharks in groups of as many as 1,000. Today most of these schools have been fished out. Like the great herds of bison that used to roam North America, they're gone.

Shark meat for sale in Europe.

Food for Thought

3 Sharks Per Second

No one knows for sure, but some shark experts estimate about 100 million sharks die on the lines and in the nets of fishermen every year. Do the math and you will see that equals 273,973 sharks killed every day, 11,416 every hour. That means three sharks die every second. In the time it's taken you to read these four sentences, about 100 more sharks have been killed.

Sharkfin

Until I read it on the menu of a Chinese restaurant in my neighborhood, I'd never heard of sharkfin soup. My friend's parents owned the Ling Nam Restaurant, so I asked him what he knew about the soup. Was it really made from shark's fins? This is what he told me. The soup, he said, originated in China more than 1000 years ago, but back then only the wealthiest people ate it. It was an expensive, luxury food like caviar, bear's paw, abalone, pangolin, turtle soup or the most prized bluefin tuna sushi and sashimi are today.

It was costly because shark fins were hard to get, and they weren't just thrown in a pot and cooked. First, they had to be prepared and this took days. Long ago, only families with full-time servants and a chef ate sharkfin soup. Being expensive and rare, my friend explained, sharkfin soup came to be seen as precious, and it became a symbol of prosperity and status in Chinese culture. Like owning a Mercedes Benz or a Rolex watch today, eating sharkfin soup made some people feel important and successful. My friend invited me to come by the Ling Nam the next day when his dad would be making some.

Preparing the Fins

Mr. Wong, my friend's dad, bought his fins ready to use in soup because preparing them takes a long time. The fins, he explained, are dried twice and cooked three times before they're eaten. Mr. Wong bought his fins from a local seafood distributor who purchased them from a fin dealer in Hong Kong, China, which imports more shark fins than any other place in the world.

The journey shark fins make from the ocean to a bowl of soup begins when a fisherman slices them off a shark, said Mr. Wong. Next, the fins are dried in the sun or sometimes in ovens. After they're dry, skin, flesh and bone, left at the base of the fin, are trimmed off. The dried fins are now boiled gently so the bone (actually a piece of cartilage) and the skin can be removed. Fins that aren't white are sometimes bleached with hydrogen peroxide. The fins are now ready to be cooked a second time. They're boiled up to eight hours with ginger, onions, spring onions and Chinese wine to remove any "fishy" taste. Finally, the fins are again dried and packaged to ship to restaurants and shops throughout the world.

A bowl of sharkfin soup next to a package of the dried noodle-like strands of cartilage.

Its Popularity has Exploded

Thousands of fins dry on racks in Taiwan.

Soup

A man prepares fins in Taiwan.

It's the inside of the fin, made of noodle-like strands of cartilage called **needles**, that chefs want. Mr. Wong handed me a few fin needles he had soaking in a bowl. I could see why they got their name. They looked just like sewing needles except they were clear and both ends tapered to a point. Between my fingers the fin needles were stretchy like a rubber band. I tried one. It was rubbery and broke apart when I chewed it, but it had no taste. I must have looked puzzled because Mr. Wong smiled.

Making the Soup

The secret of making sharkfin soup, he said, is its broth. The fin needles don't add any taste to the soup. They just absorb other flavors. Sharkfin soup actually gets its flavor from chicken, ham and pork loin. These meats are simmered in water for up to eight hours, and their broth is what gives sharkfin soup its taste. The needles just add texture.

A Food for Celebrations

Who eats sharkfin soup? Traditionally, Mr. Wong explained, the soup was eaten at weddings, festivals and family celebrations. But in the last 20 years, its popularity has exploded. The Chinese government used to discourage people from eating foods associated with status and wealth, but it no longer does. So as Asia's population has grown, more wealthy Asians want to eat sharkfin soup. Today, it's served in fancy Asian restaurants throughout the world. It's a food many Asians connect with success and prosperity. At the Ling Nam, Mr. Wong sold a bowl of his best sharkfin soup for US$100.

I asked Mr. Wong if he worried sharkfin soup might become so popular that we'd eat too many sharks. He said no, smiling at my question like it was silly. The oceans, he said, are too big and there are too many sharks to catch them all. Animals are here to feed people, he said. It's nature's way. The way it's been since there have been people on Earth. I didn't ask Mr. Wong any more questions or tell him what I was learning while reading about the oceans and SCUBA diving around our island. I left the Ling Nam worried about the future for sharks.

Dried Twice

Cooked 3 Times

Fins dry along a city street in Singapore.

Fewer Sharks

All living things need energy to breathe, move, reproduce and grow. Plants get energy from the sun, animals from the foods they eat. Most food energy, however, just keeps animals alive. About 90% of the food animals eat is used for breathing, moving, reproducing and searching for more food. Only 10% helps them grow bigger. So, in simple terms, to grow just 1 kilo, most animals need to eat 10 kilos of food.

Look at the energy pyramid on the right. It takes about 10 kilos of tuna to make one kilo of oceanic whitetip shark. But, in order to make 10 kilos of tuna, the tuna ate roughly 100 kilos of squid. That 100 kilos of squid ate about 1,000 kilos of krill (a small shrimp-like animal) and the 1,000 kilos of krill ate as much as 10,000 kilos of phytoplankton. Phytoplankton are tiny ocean plants that produce the energy that fuels nearly all marine ecosystems.

SQUID 100 KG

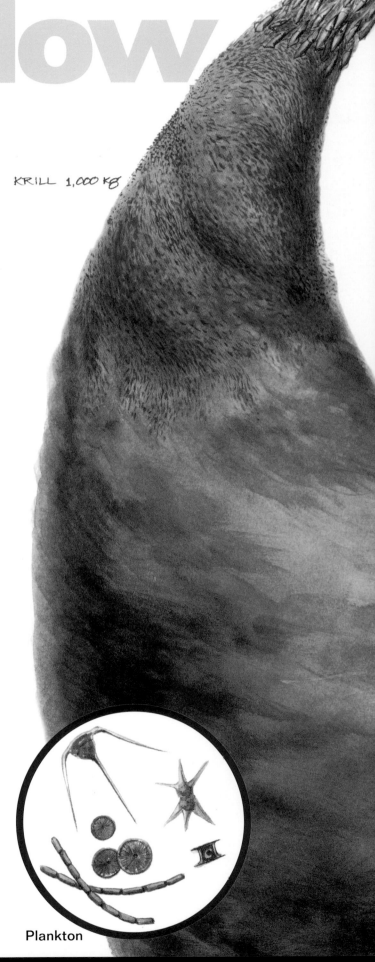

KRILL 1,000 KG

A frilled shark.

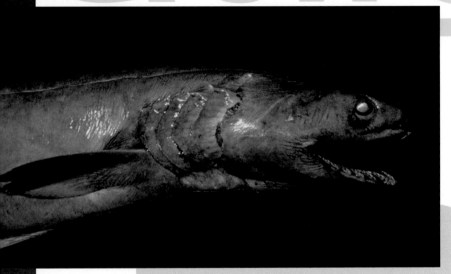

Sharks Reproduce Slowly

Some fish reproduce at a young age and lay thousands (even millions) of eggs each year. When their populations decline, they can sometimes rebuild their numbers in just a few years if the fishing stops. Sharks can't. Here are three reasons why:

Most sharks are pregnant for a long time. It is not uncommon for a shark to be pregnant for 9 to 12 months. The frilled shark seems to hold the record. It's pregnant for at least three and a half years!

Sharks have only a few babies at one time. The thresher shark has 2 to 4 pups every year, the great white about 7. The Spiny Dogfish has about 20 every other year.

Like humans, sharks are quite old before they can reproduce. A whale shark female doesn't have babies until she's 25 years old and 9 meters long. A female hammerhead won't reproduce until she's 15. The tiger shark on this page is 14–16 years old. Because sharks wait longer to reproduce, there can be years when no new sharks are born if all of a population's large sharks have been caught.

This tiger shark and her newborn pup were caught by researchers in the Bahamas. Both were released alive.

Plankton

Can't Catch as Many

TUNA 10 Kg

Little Litters

My dad has a garden where he grows hot peppers and other vegetables. One of my chores is watering and weeding his garden. Every week I pull out the weeds, and every week they grow back. Sharks, I've learned, don't grow as fast as weeds. They live a long time and have few babies. While many dogs can have puppies before age two, some big sharks don't have pups until they're in their teens or twenties. Maturing later in life was never a problem for sharks because, until recently, they had few enemies and usually lived long lives.

Today things are different. Sharks are no longer the top ocean predator. We are. On a United Nations website I learned that more fishermen are fishing more of the oceans than ever before. As they catch all the sharks in one region, fishermen travel to more remote places that haven't been fished. This is possible today because boats are faster, bigger and can stay out at sea longer. Ships have freezers, and fish can be frozen onboard. Sonar, satellites and other sophisticated fish-finding equipment help today's fishermen locate their prey. When I put these things together, and consider how fast the human population is growing, I understand how it's possible to catch too many sharks.

PHYTOPLANKTON 10,000 Kg

The oceanic whitetip shark indirectly eats every single creature in this illustration to gain just one kilo. That's one reason why, compared to other creatures, there are fewer sharks in the oceans. It takes so much food to grow them that the sea can't support as many.

Food for Thought

In 1800 most boats had sails, and there were 1 billion people on the Earth. By 1930 the world's population had doubled, but fishermen still caught few sharks. But, by 1960, things were changing. Boats had giant freezers and engines and there were 3 billion people on the planet. Already some populations of sharks were declining. By 1975 the world's population had grown to 4 billion. It hit 5 billion in 1987. Today it's more than 6 billion. By 2011 it is expected to pass 7 billion. By 2023, 8 billion. By 2035, 9 billion . . . .

6 Billion in 2000

Population in Billions

10
8
6
4
2
0

1750 1800 1850 1900 1930 2000 2050 2100 2150

Years

The deck of a shark finning boat in Costa Rica.

Waste

Killed for Only Their Fins

To feed the demand for soup, millions of sharks are killed every month just for their fins. This grey reef shark was finned at Ari Atoll in the Maldives, a group of islands south of India.

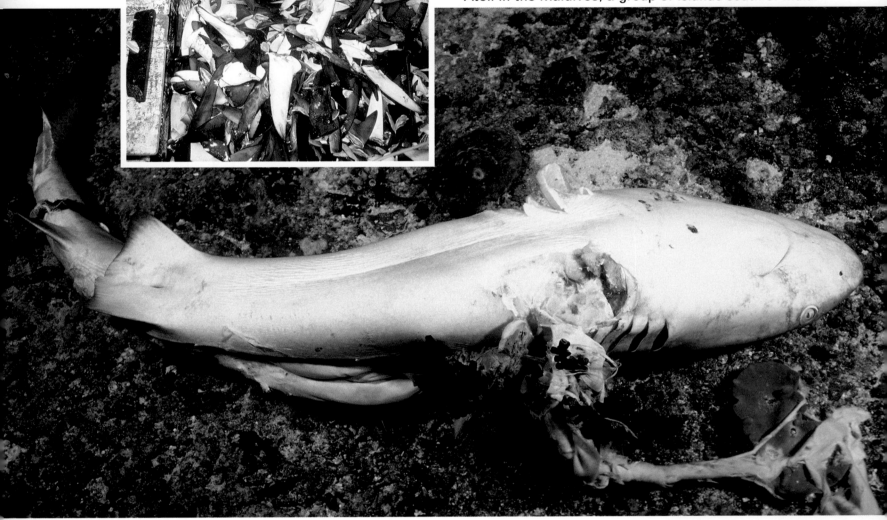

Profit

Huge Profits

Fins at a Chinese store in the U.S. city of Seattle cost US$878/kg ($399/lb). In Hong Kong, Taipei, Singapore and other Asian cities, prepared fins like these can sell for even more. Fishermen don't get as much. In Costa Rica and Indonesia fishermen are only paid US$30-100/kg ($14-45/lb) for fins. West African fishermen get as little as US$6-30/kg ($3-14/lb). The enormous profit made from selling fins makes finning a lucrative business for fin dealers and fishing business owners.

Baby Sharks Too

Finning is so profitable that even small sharks and baby sharks are finned. This picture shows tiny shark fins from Indonesia, the world's leading supplier of fins.

Killing Sharks for their Fins

I saw my first finned shark with my mom. We were diving over a coral reef, and I was admiring a scorpionfish, a master of camouflage about as big as a sneaker. Scorpionfish can change their color to match the rocks on the bottom. They're ambush hunters. They lie still, waiting for small fish and shrimp to swim within gulping distance.

Suddenly, a long white object a few meters away caught my eye. Unlike the scorpionfish, its creamy white color stood out against the rocky grey bottom. I swam over. It was a small, grey reef shark. It had been **finned**, which means its dorsal fins, pectoral fins and the bottom half of its tail fin had all been cut off, and its body had been thrown back into the water. A fisherman had probably finned this one the night before.

I picked it up. Feather-light, I could barely feel it in my hands. It felt strange to hold a shark. It still looked alive. There were no cuts in its body except for where its fins had been sliced off with a knife. Some sharks are finned after they've died in a net or on a line, but many are finned alive. For those thrown back alive it's not a second chance. Sharks aren't like a sea star (starfish) that can re-grow an arm that's been lost. Even though a finned shark may still have the top half of its tail when it's dumped back in the water, it cannot swim anymore. It either suffocates because it can't breathe, or it bleeds to death.

Looking back at the scorpionfish, I thought of the thousands of extraordinary creatures that live on coral reefs. They're part of what scientists call the diversity of life or **biodiversity**. If you think of a coral reef as a colorful, handmade carpet that's been woven together, the scorpionfish and the grey reef shark are only single threads. Pull out enough threads and any carpet not only becomes less beautiful, it also becomes weaker.

I wondered who would eat the fins of the shark I was holding. Would that person know how his bowl of soup had impacted this reef? Probably not. Today we know so little about where our food comes from that few people see the connection between what they eat and what happens to animals and the environment.

Food for Thought

Because records were kept, we know that in 1998 Hawaiian longline fishermen targeting tuna and swordfish kept about 61,000 sharks. Nearly 99 percent of these were killed for only their fins. Why? Shark bodies aren't as valuable as fins, and Hawaiian fishermen didn't want to fill up the limited freezer space on their boats with sharks when tuna and swordfish are worth so much more. Few nations require their fishermen to keep detailed records, but some scientists suspect that the wide-ranging tuna and swordfishing fishing fleets of Japan, Taiwan, Korea, Indonesia, China and other countries may kill a similar proportion of sharks for just their fins.

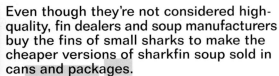

Even though they're not considered high-quality, fin dealers and soup manufacturers buy the fins of small sharks to make the cheaper versions of sharkfin soup sold in cans and packages.

Finning

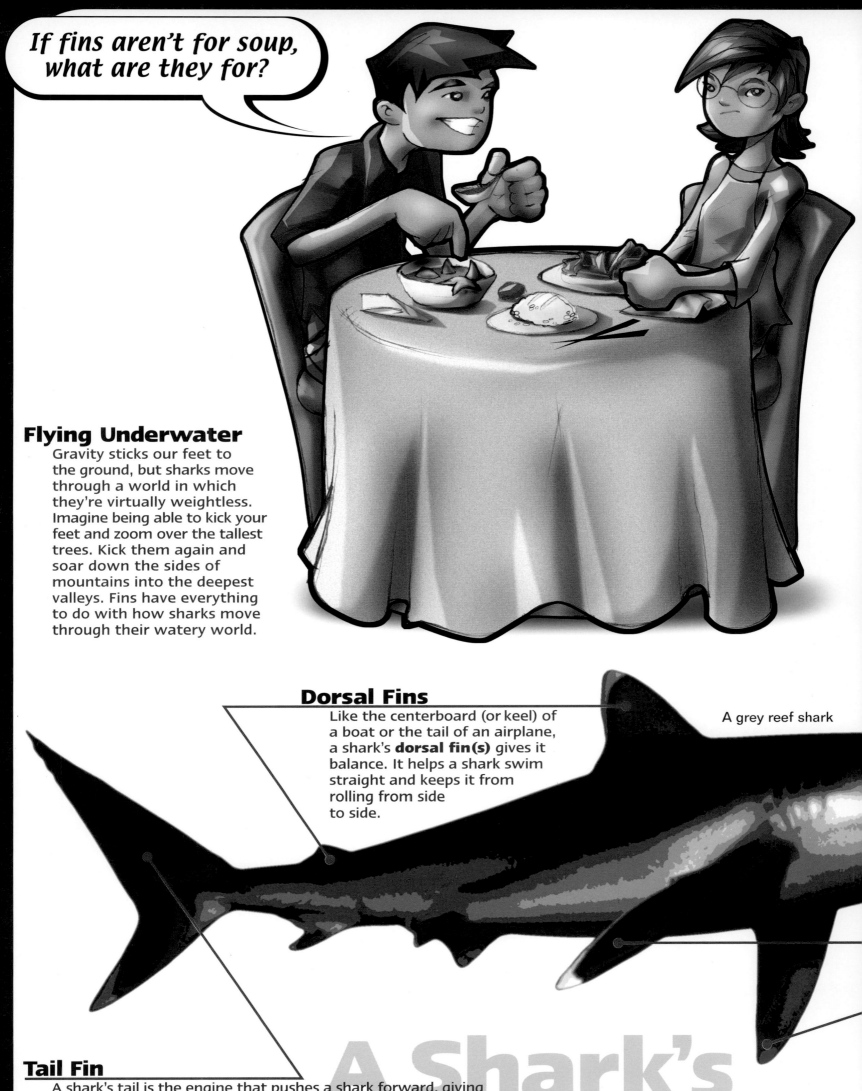

If fins aren't for soup, what are they for?

Flying Underwater

Gravity sticks our feet to the ground, but sharks move through a world in which they're virtually weightless. Imagine being able to kick your feet and zoom over the tallest trees. Kick them again and soar down the sides of mountains into the deepest valleys. Fins have everything to do with how sharks move through their watery world.

Dorsal Fins

Like the centerboard (or keel) of a boat or the tail of an airplane, a shark's **dorsal fin(s)** gives it balance. It helps a shark swim straight and keeps it from rolling from side to side.

A grey reef shark

Tail Fin

A shark's tail is the engine that pushes a shark forward, giving it power and speed. The tail, also called a **caudal fin**, is divided into two halves called **lobes**. A shark's backbone extends to nearly the tip of the top lobe giving it incredible strength. This tail design shoves a shark slightly downward while it's swimming. To balance this force, a shark uses its pectoral fins and the upward sloping underside of its snout to keep level.

A Shark's Motor

If Not for Soup...

Soon after I saw the finned shark, I went with my mom to a small market in a village near our house. There, on some woven mats, the wives of fishermen had set out the evening's catch. To my surprise there was also a small shark. I had never seen one at this market before. I stared at it and suddenly felt sad. It was then that I realized I had come to see sharks differently.

I saw them as vulnerable, in need of my protection. I felt the way I do when I see a bird fly into a window and knock itself senseless or my baby brother falls and needs my help to get up.

"How about some shark?" my mom asked, waking me from my thoughts.

"No thanks, mom."

"What's the matter? You don't eat shark anymore either?" She smiled.

"Nope," I said, "not any more."

We didn't buy any fish that day. Although my mom said none of the fish looked good, I think she sensed how I felt. Looking back, I see that it was on that day that I started respecting sharks as wild animals. Getting to know fish in their natural environment, I've realized they have a purpose beyond just being food for people. To swim with a shark is to see that it's more than just an ingredient in soup or a piece of meat for someone's dinner.

This was an important discovery for me. Before, when I only thought of fish as people food, I didn't think to wonder how sharks die, or care about how many are killed. While I don't think there is anything wrong with people eating sharks and other fish, I am concerned about how many are dying. I left the market knowing I wanted to help sharks, but not knowing if there was anything one person could do.

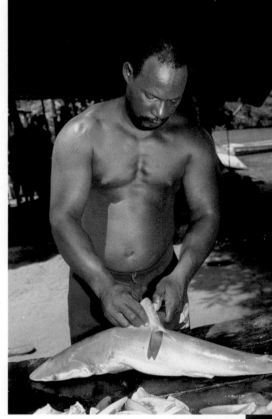

A man fins a juvenile shark at a market in Trinidad.

Steering

Pectoral Fins

To steer and turn, a shark adjusts its **pectoral fins** up or down. This lets it cruise to the surface or dive. Moving its pectoral fins independently—one up, the other down—lets it turn in any direction it chooses. The fins on the front of a submarine work in a similar way.

The shape of a shark's pectoral fins also helps it swim level. Like the wings of a plane, a shark's pectoral fins have a slight curve to their upper surface and are flat on the bottom. This shape forces water to move more quickly over the top of the fins and more slowly underneath. The slower-moving water creates more pressure under the fin and actually pushes the shark forward and up. This force is called **lift**.

Lift

Food for Thought

A shark's fins are only 5% of its entire body weight. Ninety-five percent of a shark is wasted when it's finned.

23

Three Different Tails

Three sharks, three different tails,
dorsal fins in three different places. Why?

The streamlined blacktip reef shark spends its time swimming above a coral reef and chasing fish in open water. It needs a tail built for all-day swimming and a dorsal fin in the middle of its back to keep it balanced.

The flatter angel shark spends its time camouflaged on the sea floor waiting to ambush small fish that swim too close. Because a bigger one would drag in the sand, its tail has a small bottom lobe. It needs no big dorsal fin to keep it balanced. Instead it has two smaller dorsal fins close to its tail to help give it a quick burst of speed when it surprises its prey.

The nurse shark has a tail and dorsal fins that are a compromise between the other two sharks because it spends some time swimming and some time lying on the bottom. Its first dorsal fin is big enough to provide stability, while the second fin closer to the tail gives it a quick burst of speed. The long top lobe of its tail and tiny bottom lobe enable the nurse shark to lie on the sea floor and maneuver in and out of caves and reef crevices where it hunts lobsters, octopus and slow swimming fish.

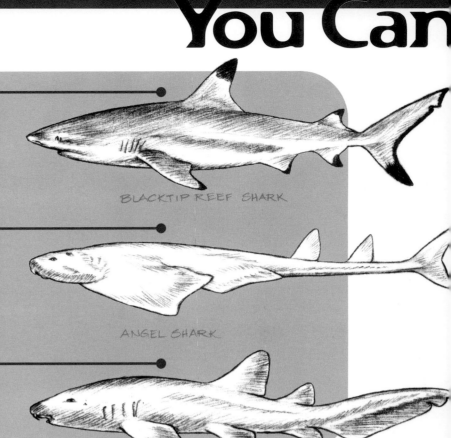

BLACKTIP REEF SHARK

ANGEL SHARK

NURSE SHARK

and by its Fins...

MAKO SHARK

SALMON SHARK

BIGEYE TUNA

Like the oceans' speediest fish, the fastest sharks have tails shaped like boomerangs with two lobes that are tall and thin and nearly equal in size.

A thresher shark in the Philippines.

but Not Every

MANTA RAY

SWORDFISH

KSPENCER
2002©

Judge a Shark by its Tail...

When I was younger, I spent hours looking at books with pictures of sea creatures and drawing them. The strange and secretive ones grabbed my attention the most. Moray eels amazed and frightened me. Nearly blind, they live in caves in the reef and hunt at night, using only their sense of smell. Don't ever, I read, put your hand in a hole in a coral reef. There could be a moray eel in there. The octopus also captured my imagination. Clever, intelligent and able to squirt out a cloud of ink and make a getaway by confusing eels and other predators. How about narwhals? What are their long tusks for? And the giant squid? No one has ever seen one alive. In my dreams, I'd imagine sperm whales diving into the ocean's depths and fighting them. All these animals still remain a great mystery to me.

When it comes to sharks, the thresher has always fascinated me. The top lobe of a thresher shark's tail can be as long as its body—up to 3 meters! Why do they have such incredibly long tails? No one knows for sure, because nobody has ever seen a thresher use its tail. Some scientists think threshers may slap the surface of the water with their tails to scare schools of small fish into tight balls so they can more easily catch them. Others have written that, like orcas (killer whales), threshers may whack fish senseless with their tails. When orcas do this, they swim back slowly to eat the dazed and dead fish. Do threshers do it too?

Once at the deep edge of a coral reef, I saw a thresher. I felt like the astronauts did who first walked on the moon. Threshers are usually so shy that few divers ever see them. Even though I had read about them a hundred times and drawn dozens of pictures of them, I couldn't stop admiring this extraordinary shark as it swam past me. I kept hoping it would find a school of fish nearby and show me how it uses its tail.

Food for Thought

From a distance, do tuna and billfish mistake the white-tipped fins of oceanic whitetip sharks for a school of small fish and swim quickly toward them? Scientists have a hunch that this might be how this big shark catches faster-swimming prey.

Fin Belongs to a Shark.

SPOTTED DOLPHIN

TIGER SHARK

A Mouthful of Tools

To bite an apple, we use our front teeth. Their bottom edges are thin and break through the apple's skin easily, letting us tear out a chunk. But we don't chew with our front teeth. They're not designed for that. To chew, our tongues push the apple to the back of our mouths where our flatter molars crush and grind it. Our teeth are specialized. Their different designs are adapted to different jobs. Sharks also have specialized teeth that tell us how and what they eat and where they fit into the ocean's ecosystems.

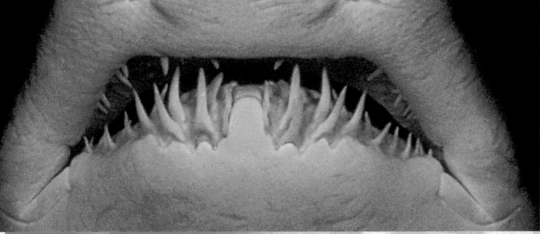

Grinding

Teeth for Stabbing

The long, pointed, slender teeth of this sand tiger shark are good for grabbing fast-moving prey that darts around and doesn't have to be bitten into pieces. With teeth like these, it's not surprising that sand tigers gulp down squid and fish without chewing.

Teeth for Grinding

While its front teeth are pointy and grip its prey, the rear teeth of the Port Jackson shark have a surface more like our molars. These teeth are for crushing the shells of crabs and clams.

Stabbing

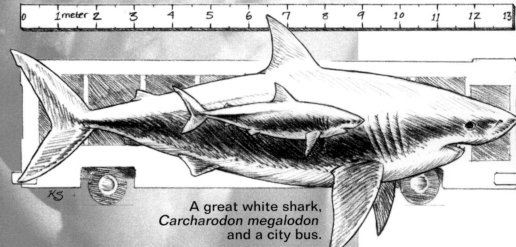

A great white shark, *Carcharodon megalodon* and a city bus.

Cutting

Teeth for Cutting

Big, flat and triangular, with edges like a saw blade, the top teeth of a great white shark are designed to slice. This is so they can mortally wound seals and other big marine mammals with one bite. A great white's bottom teeth are sharper and narrower. Their job is to grip prey, while the top teeth cut.

Shark Teeth

Imagine a shark's tooth so big it nearly covers your hand. Better still, dream about the shark that owned it. After opening a package my grandmother sent me for my birthday, this is just what I did. Inside was a fossilized tooth of *Carcharodon megalodon*, a close relative of the great white and one of the biggest sharks that ever lived.

While ancient sharks did leave behind some skeletons, fossilized teeth are the most commonly found clues that they were here. This is because shark skeletons are made of cartilage (not bone like dinosaur skeletons). Cartilage usually rots too quickly to become fossilized. With a little imagination and information about the tooth shape, skeletons and eating habits of today's sharks, people can make good guesses about what ancient sharks were like.

In a book, I read that *Carcharodon megalodon's* teeth are similar to those of a great white shark, except Carchy's teeth were a lot larger. So much bigger (up to 15 cm) that scientists estimate this ancient shark grew as long as a bus (12-13 meters) but weighed more (12-14 tonnes). Carchy's tail would have been about 4 meters tall and its dorsal fin nearly 2 meters.

Like the great white, *Carcharodon megalodon* probably ate marine mammals and was a top ocean predator. The size, shape and sharp edges of its teeth suggest this, but here's a clue that's even better. In the fossilized backbones of some ancient whales, scientists have found the broken-off teeth of *Carcharodon megalodon*.

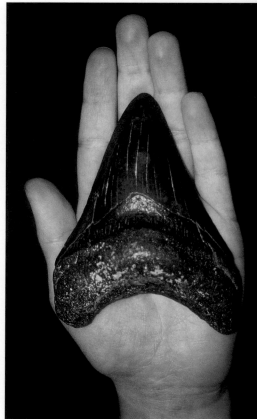

A fossilized *Carcharodon megalodon* tooth.

Teeth on a Conveyor Belt

Behind the first row of teeth in a shark's jaw you will see many more. They line up, one behind the other. This nifty design lets a shark quickly replace teeth that break or fall out. A shark's tooth moves into place much faster than it takes a kid to get a new tooth. This is because sharks' teeth are not attached to their jawbones, but to their skin. The skin covering the jaw works like a conveyor belt rotating new teeth into place every 7 to 30 days. Like chefs who constantly sharpen their knives, this system gives sharks the sharp tools they need to survive.

Food for Thought

Normally, people get 52 teeth in a lifetime. Some sharks may get as many as 30,000. The first 20 teeth humans get are baby teeth that start falling out by age 5 or 6 to make room for permanent ones. Sharks lose and replace teeth every few weeks, which is why on some beaches and in some layers of sediment you can find a lot of fossilized sharks' teeth.

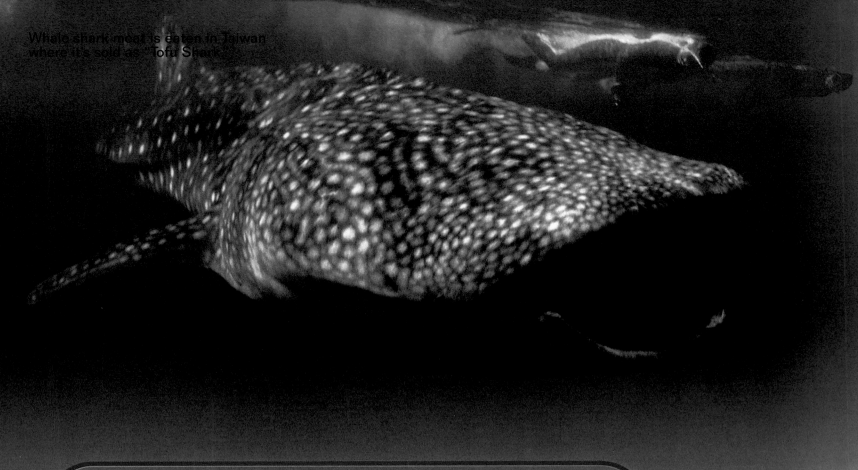

Whale shark meat is eaten in Taiwan where it's sold as "Tofu Shark."

Hunting the Hunters

The tiny cookie cutter shark, no bigger than your forearm, lives in deep water in the middle of the ocean where there is no place to hide. It doesn't swim quickly either, but somehow it manages to bite round cookie-shaped chunks out of the ocean's super-predators, fast hunters like bluefin tuna and swordfish and swift, powerful mammals like dolphins and porpoises.

How does it do it? No one knows for sure. Some scientists think it attracts bigger fish by pretending to be a cleaner fish (a small fish that eats parasites off big ones). Others suspect it produces light (**bioluminescence**) on its belly and around its neck to lure victims close. Then, with a burst of speed, this mega-mosquito grabs hold of its prey. With top teeth that grip and bottom teeth that cut, a cookie cutter shark bites out a round plug of flesh by slowly rotating its body in a circle.

A dolphin with a cookie cutter bite wound.

Big teeth for a small shark. A cookie cutter's mouth.

Seal and Slurp

Nurse sharks can use their lips to create a seal over crevices in a coral reef. Then, like a vacuum cleaner, they suck up small fish, shrimp, lobsters and shellfish. Divers say the noise they make sounds like a nursing baby. This may be how they got their name.

A nurse shark eating a lobster.

Eating

Soon after my birthday, Jackie and I swam with the biggest fish alive today, one that grows bigger than *Carcharodon megalodon* ever did: a whale shark. We were snorkeling close to shore when one swam by with its mouth wide open.

We had nothing to fear. Whale sharks are filter feeders. Water flows into their mouths and comes out their gill slits, passing through comb-like structures called **gill rakers** that strain out the plankton and small fish a whale shark eats.

From above, the whale shark reminded me of a giant tadpole with a big head that tapered into a long slinky tail. When I was really young, I used to imagine myself walking beside the dinosaurs. I remembered those feelings swimming next to the whale shark. It was massive.

Jackie and I dove down for a closer look. One of the first things we noticed was the markings on its back—thin, white, vertical bars and spots on grey-black skin. I was surprised how well this pattern camouflaged the whale shark. It blended in with the sea floor far below.

Swimming beside the whale shark didn't seem to bother it, but even so, the slow sweeps of its tail sent it along quickly. We were kicking hard to keep up. After a while, Jackie and I slid back past the whale shark's enormous pectoral and dorsal fins. Restaurants and stores that serve sharkfin soup and sell fins sometimes pay thousands of dollars for whale shark fins, just to display them in storefront windows to attract customers.

These large fins once belonged to a whale shark or basking shark.

Next, we passed the long lines of sleek muscle that moved the whale shark's tail back and forth. Then came the tail itself, so big it seemed like it belonged to some prehistoric creature. It towered over us. Too tired to keep up any longer, we watched the whale shark disappear into the distant blue water—its tail gently waving. We didn't want the moment to end. We hoped this whale shark would avoid the many hunters waiting for it, and that we'd be lucky enough to see it again.

Food for Thought

Television shows and movies have scared people with the notion of a shark **feeding frenzy**. This is supposed to be when sharks go crazy over food, wildly ripping apart and eating anything nearby, even one another. But in nature, there is probably no such thing. Sharks observed around whale carcasses eat slowly and deliberately, avoiding one another.

Fishermen, divers and underwater photographers sometimes use bait (dead fish) to attract sharks. This is called **chumming**. In this photo, a ball of frozen fish has been lowered over the Great Barrier Reef in Australia to attract sharks for SCUBA diving tourists. Thousands of divers have safely observed sharks in this way without creating a Hollywood feeding frenzy.

Grey reef sharks over the Pacific's Bikini Atoll.

Threatened

Get Out of My Space

Sometimes, if a diver swims close to a grey reef shark it will arch its back upward. Like a dog's growl, this is a warning. "Back off or I may to bite you." Some scientists think grey reef sharks behave this way because a diver has unknowingly entered the shark's personal space.

What's a shark's personal space? It is hard to know. Just like with humans, it probably changes with every situation. Imagine you get into an elevator. If it's crowded, it's O.K. that your arm touches the person standing next to you. You're not invading his personal space. But, what if there is only one other person in the elevator? Now, if you stand so close to him that your arms touch, he may get mad because you're in his personal space.

Mistaken

To a shark, could this surfer resemble a seal or sea turtle?

A great white attacks a fur seal in South Africa.

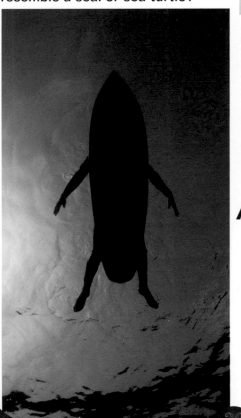

A Case of Mistaken Identity?

Sometimes swimmers and surfers look like a shark's usual prey. The photo on the left shows a person on a surfboard. To a great white shark, he might look like a seal, or to a tiger or a bull shark, like a sea turtle.

When great whites attack people they usually take just one bite and then back off. This is the same technique they use to hunt seals and sea lions —their normal prey. By shooting up from below, taking a huge, deadly bite, and then waiting for a seal to bleed to death, a great white reduces its chances of being hurt during an attack. Scientists call this the **bite and spit** strategy. Humans usually survive attacks by great whites because they're usually on their way to the hospital soon after they're bitten.

Shark Attack

Many people owned dogs on the island where Jackie and I lived. The big, brown and black ones our neighbor Mr. Becker owned were ferocious. Whenever we rode our bikes past, they growled and slobbered and threw themselves against the metal fence surrounding his yard. Surely, they would have ripped us to pieces if we ever went into their yard.

Farther down our street was Jackie's house. Her dog was as big as Mr. Becker's, but all it wanted to do was lick me. Its long shaggy tail never stopped wagging when I visited. After school, it loved to fetch the sticks we threw into the ocean.

At the end of our street lived an old man who was always working in his garden with a parrot on his shoulder and a dog that hid behind him with its tail between its legs. The man and his parrot loved to talk, but no matter how much Jackie and I called to his shy dog, it would never let us pet it.

I tell you about these dogs because what was true about them is also true about sharks. They're all different. It would have been wrong to think all the dogs on my street were as dangerous as Mr. Becker's, as friendly as Jackie's, or as shy as the old man's.

Why do sharks attack people? No one knows for sure. There's probably more than one answer to the question. Is it a case of mistaken identity? Does it only happen when sharks feel threatened? Do sharks bite because we're in "their yards?" Or do sharks sometimes attack humans because they're big, hungry predators, and we are vulnerable prey? Much probably depends on the circumstances and the species of shark.

Food for Thought

On page 15 you read that people kill about 100 million sharks each year. On average, only 6 people, worldwide, are killed each year by sharks. So, which species is more of a danger to the other?

A tiger shark.

Identity

Hunger

I'm Hungry. You're Here.

Humans don't like to think they can be the prey of any creature, but scientists suspect that some sharks occasionally attack people because they're hungry. We might not be what's usually for dinner, but they're willing to give us a try.

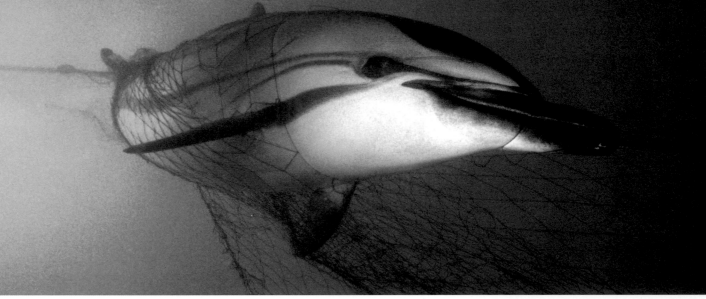

This striped dolphin drowned in a French driftnet near the Azores, islands in the North Atlantic.

Gillnets

Gillnets are walls of netting. They either hang from the surface of the sea or float up from the bottom. Some are anchored in one place. Others, allowed to drift with the current, are called **driftnets**. Driftnets can be several kilometers long and hang from the ocean surface to a depth of 40 meters. Driftnets are left in the water for 6-24 hours at a time. Each day and night, fishermen set thousands of kilometers of driftnets in the oceans.

Tuna, swordfish, and squid may be what commercial fishermen are after, but driftnets, made of thin, strong, plastic line, tangle and capture anything that tries to swim through them. Most creatures can't see the nets underwater, where there is less light. For this reason gillnets are said to be **indiscriminate**, which means they catch everything that becomes entangled in them, not just the fish fishermen want.

A dead sandbar shark on a longline in the Philippines.

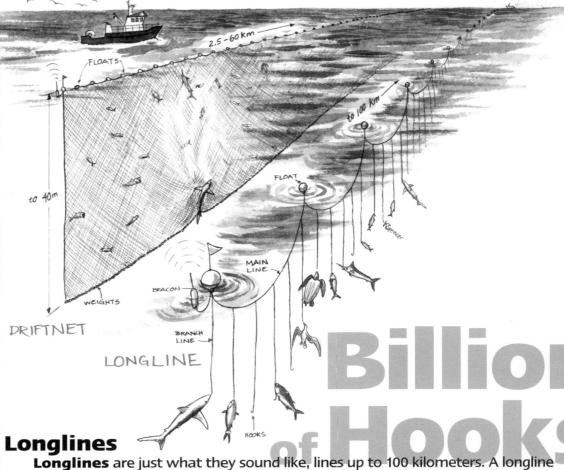

Longlines

Longlines are just what they sound like, lines up to 100 kilometers. A longline itself is made of a single, plastic, main line strong enough to lift a piano. Thousands of shorter lines—tied to hooks and baited with squid, mackerel or other fish—can be attached to the main line. Sometimes even sharks are cut up for bait to catch other sharks. Fishermen in Asia and Africa have been known to bait their lines with dolphin meat to catch sharks for their valuable fins.

Like gillnets, longlines are left in the oceans for 6-24 hours. A boat usually sets many lines in the water at the same time, letting it fish 10,000 or more hooks at once. Boats and crew fish day and night—retrieving old lines and setting new ones over many square kilometers of ocean. Fishing boats are able to find their longlines and driftnets because the floats that support them carry radio transmitters that broadcast their positions.

It is estimated that billions of longline hooks are set in the oceans every year primarily to catch tuna, swordfish and sharks. Like gillnets, longlines are indiscriminate. Any animal large enough to bite a fist-sized hook is caught.

Fishing

The more I read, the more I discovered that populations of sharks and other sea creatures are declining all over the world, and they have been for many years. The main reason is too much fishing, and there is actually a name for this problem. It is called **overfishing**.

At first it seemed impossible. How could we overfish places as big as the oceans? Understanding who catches fish and how fish are caught today helped me answer this question. You probably know how a hook and line works —catching one fish at a time. Sharks and other fish are still caught this way by **artisanal** fishermen, generally poor people, men and women, who catch fish to feed their own families or sell at a local market. **Recreational** fishermen, people who fish for fun, also use hooks and lines to catch fish.

But most seafood sold in restaurants and at big city markets is caught by people who fish for a business. These **commercial fishermen** fish to make money and earn a living. How do commercial fishermen catch sharks, tuna, swordfish, shrimp and other sea creatures we eat? Think big. Some commercial fishermen use nets large enough to scoop up entire neighborhoods —buildings and all. Imagine lines as long as highways. Commercial fishermen still use hooks to catch fish, but today they use thousands at a time. There are four basic kinds of fishing gear commercial fishermen use to catch most of the seafood we eat: gillnets, longlines, trawls and purse seines.

Walls of Netting

Overfishing

Food for Thought

This albatross is about to drown. Look carefully and you'll see a fishing line in its beak leading into the water. It has grabbed one of the baited hooks on a longline being set for swordfish behind a Brazilian fishing boat. The swordfish are exported to the United States, but few consumers know the full cost of their swordfish steaks. Every year, hundreds of thousands of seabirds die this way. At least 64 species of seabirds are killed by longlines worldwide. Of these, 23 are threatened with extinction.

The haul from a Mexican trawl. Fishermen will pick through the catch, put the shrimp in the baskets, and then shovel everything else overboard. Most of these discarded creatures will be dead.

Trawls

Trawls are bag-shaped nets pulled by boats called **trawlers**. Some trawls are big enough to swallow a dozen or more jet airplanes. Many trawls, like those used to catch shrimp, are dragged over the ocean floor. This is called bottom trawling, and it's one of the most destructive and wasteful forms of fishing. It destroys ocean floor habitat, and it kills far more living things than it catches.

How does a bottom trawl work? Big metal doors hold the net open while metal chains just in front of the net's mouth drag across the ocean floor. The chains frighten fish as well as shrimp up off the bottom so they swim into the mouth of the net, but the chains also scrape the sea floor like a bulldozer. A single drag of a trawl knocks over piles of rocks, breaks sponges and corals, and tears up marine life attached to the bottom. Scientists have discovered that bottom trawling reduces the variety of species on the seafloor, and because it leaves so many animals homeless, it makes it impossible for many populations to rebuild themselves.

Bottom trawls are also black holes for all the other sea creatures that enter them. In some trawl fisheries for shrimp or prawns, for every one tonne (1000 kilograms) of shrimp netted, up to 10 tonnes of other marine life are caught. Almost all these other creatures die in the trawl net or on the deck of the boat. About two thirds of these unwanted animals are fish including young sharks and rays. The other third are creatures that live on or near the sea floor like crabs, octopus, corals and sponges. Sea turtles are also killed in trawls. Scientists estimate that 150,000 or more sea turtles drown each year in shrimp trawls. Like longlines and gillnets, trawls are indiscriminate.

TRAWLER

Dragged

METAL DOORS

HEALTHY SEAFLOOR HABITAT

A ray is one of many creatures caught by this shrimp trawl in the Gulf of California. Most people don't realize how much other sea life is wasted trawling for shrimp.

More Fishing

Purse Seines

Many fish like to travel in tightly-packed schools, which enables a boat called a **purse seiner** to catch them easily. These schools are usually spotted on the surface by a lookout aboard the boat, from an airplane or helicopter, or by fishermen using fish-detecting sonar on the ship. To circle and catch a school of fish, a seiner pulls a wall of netting all the way around the school with the help of a small speedboat that holds on to one end of the net. This prevents fish from escaping in any direction except down, but that exit is quickly closed as the bottom of the net is pulled shut. This turns the net, called a **purse seine**, into a giant bowl (or purse) with its opening floating at the surface and the fish inside. Escape is now impossible, and the net is pulled aboard the seiner.

It is sometimes possible for purse seines to avoid catching unwanted fish and other sea creatures. In the 1970s and 80s, tuna fishermen using purse seines killed hundreds of thousands of dolphins. After consumers complained, fishing companies and fishermen changed the nets and the way they used them to reduce the number of dolphins they killed. But while new seining methods have reduced the catch of dolphins, they sometimes kill other sea creatures. In 1993-94 an estimated 6.6 million animals including sharks, sea turtles, and juvenile billfish and tuna were also caught and killed in purse seines. The bodies of these unwanted creatures were dumped back into the ocean.

No Escape

Over the Ocean Floor

Food for Thought

A piece of sea floor about twice the size of the United States (not including Alaska) is trawled every year. This area is roughly equal to half of the world's **continental shelf**, the shallow ocean floor surrounding all the continents.

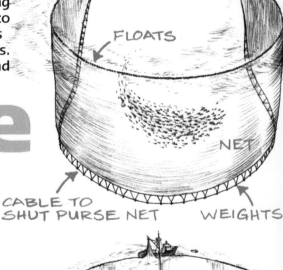

SPEEDBOAT

SCHOOL OF FISH

PURSE SEINER

FLOATS

NET

CABLE TO SHUT PURSE NET

WEIGHTS

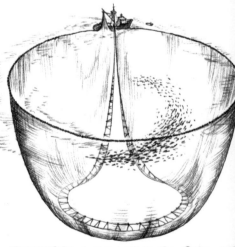

BOTTOM OF NET CLOSING

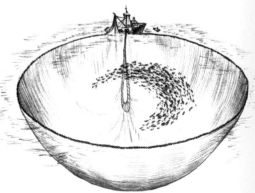

NET CLOSED

TRAWL NET

SEA CREATURES CAUGHT IN SMALL MESH AT NARROW END OF NET

DAMAGED SEAFLOOR HABITAT

Purse Seine Bycatch

What else gets caught, killed and discarded every time a Pacific Ocean tuna boat sets its enormous purse seine around some logs, placed in the water by fishermen to attract yellowfin tuna?

1 sea turtle   1 billfish
12 other large bony fish
21 sharks and rays
190 wahoo
800 other small fish
382 mahi-mahi (dolphin fish)
428 triggerfish
15,620 small tunas

These numbers are averages.

Thrown

Away

This olive ridley sea turtle was caught on a longline set for mahi-mahi in Costa Rican waters. It's estimated that 40,000 sea turtles are hooked and die on longlines each year. The mahi-mahi are exported to the United States.

The world's biggest reptiles, leatherback sea turtles are on the verge of extinction. Many are caught as bycatch on longlines. In 1980 an estimated 91,000 adult female leatherbacks came ashore to nest on beaches in Costa Rica, Nicaragua, and Mexico. Only 1,690 did in 1999. In Terranganu, Malaysia, 3,103 came ashore to nest in 1968. Only two returned in 1994.

How Much?

How Much is Wasted?

It's not easy to picture how much sea life is wasted in order to put seafood on our plates, but here's a comparison. All the debris from the World Trade Center buildings, destroyed in 2001 in New York City, weighed about 1.65 million tonnes. The amount of bycatch every year is more than 12 times this. Picture 24 World Trade Center towers piled one on top of another. This stack of towers would reach more than 10,000 meters into the sky—higher than Mt. Everest.

The New York Times newspaper said it took 108,444 dump truck loads to haul away the debris—broken pieces of concrete, glass and steel—left by the collapse of the two giant skyscrapers. Using the same size trucks, it would take 1,314,473 loads to haul away a year's worth of the world's bycatch.

Because their meat spoils quickly, blue sharks like this one caught on a longline set for swordfish are usually finned and discarded.

Bycatch

Imagine a deer hunter whose hunting equipment is so indiscriminate that every time he kills an adult deer, he also kills some fawns, a few dozen wild birds, a bear, a tiger, a couple lions, some rabbits, mice and moles, an elephant and buckets full of bugs. Since the hunter only wants the adult deer, which he can sell, he leaves everything else in piles on the ground. His big hunting machines also damage the environment—plowing through forests and fields—leaving a path of destruction behind them. For years the hunter has hunted deer this way. He regrets that his machines kill other things, "but the forest is a big place," he thinks, "and this is how I make a living."

What would you say about this hunter? "The guy is crazy!" That's what I would say. "People shouldn't kill things and waste them. It's wrong."

Of course I made this up, but I've discovered a similar, true story takes place in our oceans everyday. The nets and longlines that commercial fishermen use are so indiscriminate that each year they catch and kill at least 20 million metric tonnes of unwanted marine wildlife (1 metric tonne = 1,000 kilos = 2,200 pounds). Do the math. You'll discover that each year commercial fisherman dump back into the ocean more than 20 billion kilos or 44 billion pounds of sea creatures they catch but don't want. Sadly, most of these animals are dead.

What gets discarded? Just name a sea creature. Sharks, skates and rays, young tunas, billfish and thousands of other kinds of fish are all tossed out. Hundreds of thousands of sea turtles, sea birds, dolphins, whales, sea lions, seals, sea stars, jelly fish, sponges and corals also die after being caught by commercial fishing nets and longlines. These forgotten casualties of our commercial fishing practices are called **bycatch**. Each year more than one quarter of everything commercial fishermen catch is bycatch.

Remember the hunter? Imagine he sold his deer meat at a restaurant or market where your family bought food. Would you buy it if you knew that his hunting machines were destroying the forests and the creatures that live there?

What died so I could eat this?

Food for Thought

In 1996, for every 22 swordfish caught in the California driftnet fishery, one dolphin or whale, three sharks and six other fish were killed.

Can We Share Fish

The demand for fish in wealthier nations impacts more than sharks. Because they have caught most of the valuable fish in the waters close to their homes, commercial fishing boats from wealthier countries now scour African waters for all kinds of seafood. This impacts Africans. Today, they must fish longer to catch fewer, smaller fish. Above, two African men trade little fish on a beach.

One day my dad came home from work and asked me if I wanted to come with him on a business trip to Taipei.

"Taipei?" I said, surprised by his question. "Where's that?"

"Taiwan, of course."

"Yeah," I said, "but why would I want to go to . . . . Where are you going?"

"Taipei," he said, turning to hang up his coat and put away his briefcase. "Well, if you change your mind," he said, still looking away, "let me know. There's a conference there about sharks. I just figured a kid interested in them might want to find out what experts from all over the world have to say about sharks."

I packed my bag. A week later we landed in Taiwan. My dad dropped me off at the conference each day while he went to his meetings. I was the only kid there, but it was in a big auditorium, and I found a seat by myself. I soon learned that people everywhere are concerned about sharks. Almost everyone said we're catching too many. To meet the demand for sharkfin soup and for other fish, the commercial fishing fleets of wealthy nations are catching so much that little is left for poorer people who live in fishing communities throughout the world. Some of these communities, I learned, have their own cultural and economic ties to sharks.

The conference speakers left me puzzling over many questions. How can we share sharks? Is it possible when it seems there's not enough for everyone to have as many as they want?

Sharkfin soup is a part of Chinese culture, but sharks and shark fishing also have roots in other cultures and communities. I couldn't stop thinking that sharkfin soup is only eaten by wealthy people who have many food choices. Certainly people in poorer communities in Southeast Asia, Africa and Latin America have fewer choices.

Are we sharing the oceans' resources fairly? When human populations were smaller, we didn't have to think about this, but now that we're reaching the limits of what the oceans can provide, this seems like an important question to ask.

Food Choices

Sharks and foods made from shark meat are part of the culture of the Bidjago people in the West African nation of Guinea Bissau. Young men catch them as a way of showing the adults in their community that they are worthy of greater respect and responsibility. Bidjago people also believe that sharks help them communicate with their ancestors. In the picture to the right three men wearing hammerhead shark masks wait their turn to dance at a celebration.

Fairly?

Shrinking Shark Populations

In the West African nation of The Gambia, sharks have been caught by local people since the 1960s. They dry and salt the meat and sell it throughout the region. At first their catch was small enough that it didn't appear to affect shark populations. But in the 1980s, fin traders from Taiwan and Hong Kong arrived in West Africa and things changed. Since then, so many big sharks have been caught that their populations have greatly declined. Today, local fishermen trying to keep their dried fish trade alive keep even baby sharks and rays.

Profit, The Environment and Community

The trade in fins is changing the way many artisanal fishing communities relate to one another and to the environment. Before the shark fin trade people only caught what they needed to feed their families, plus a little extra to trade. Now, with shark populations disappearing, communities compete for what remains, causing conflicts.

One occurred several years ago between the Bidjago people of the West African nation of Guinea Bissau and fishermen from Senegal. Because they had already caught most of the sharks in their home waters, Senegalese fishermen were finning sharks in the waters of Guinea Bissau where sharks were still common. Sharks and rays play an important role in the culture of the Bidjago people, and they were insulted by the waste of the Senegalese fishermen, who dumped the bodies of finned sharks back into the sea. Several Senegalese fishermen were killed in trouble that followed.

Keeping Fishermen in Debt

Even though they have become scarce, West African fishermen haven't stopped fishing for sharks because the fishermen are in **debt** (owe money) to fin traders. The traders pay West African fishermen very little for shark fins, but sell these same fins to buyers in Asia for very high prices. The huge profits allow fin traders to loan money to African fishermen who use the cash to buy gas, fix their boats and keep fishing for sharks. The fin buyers don't really care if the fishermen pay them back. What's important to the fin traders is that fishermen feel forced to continue catching sharks. To the traders, even a few shark fins are more valuable than the loans.

Small sharks and rays drying on a rack in The Gambia. Find the blue pen in the picture to estimate the size of the sharks.

Debt

Tradition

How Many Fish

Smaller

We are emptying the oceans of fish. Since 1987, the world's catch of ocean fish has been decreasing. In many regions, it's been shrinking since the early 1970s. The average size of fish being caught is also decreasing. I was surprised when I learned this. Why didn't I already know? How could there be fewer fish in the sea when there are so many at the places where my parents shop?

My own family's **affluence** or wealth has a lot to do with my ignorance. Although I don't think of myself as a "rich" person, compared to most people in the world my family has a lot of money. We shop and eat at places that provide food for other wealthy people. These markets and restaurants buy the biggest and best seafood available. Their customers can afford it. Our affluence shields us from **scarcity** (the lack of things).

Another reason I didn't know there are fewer fish today has to do with seafood farms or **aquaculture**. For centuries, people have raised fish and grown aquatic plants to eat and use in making other products. Many

The average weight of a swordfish caught before 1963 was 121 kilos (266 pounds). By 1970 it was half that. Today the average swordfish caught weighs only 41 kilos (90 pounds). These juvenile fish are too young to have ever reproduced.

Our Oceans

100 Years Ago

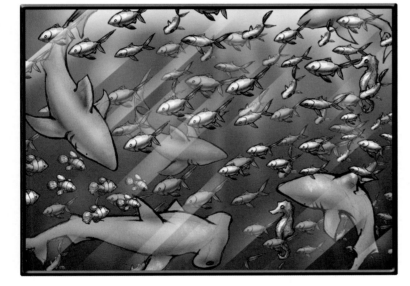

25 Years Ago

Fewer

In Great Britain some fish in "fish and chips" is advertised as being "rock salmon," which is just a made up name for a shark called the spiny dogfish.

Eating Little Fish

Today, fishermen catch large numbers of baitfish—smaller fish that used to be eaten by only bigger fish, sea birds and sea mammals. In the picture at right are Danish fishermen with a haul of sand eels. With almost all the populations of larger fish in their home waters gone, some European fishermen now target sand eels, which aren't eaten by humans, but are ground into meal (food) for farm animals. Scientists have a term to describe the practice of catching smaller and smaller fish after the larger ones have been overfished: **fishing down the food web**. What will be left after we've caught all the smaller fish? And, what will bigger fish, seals, dolphins and seabirds eat?

n the Sea?

saltwater species are grown today in ponds, tanks, and cages made of netting that hang along the shore. Since 1987, the amount of seafood grown by aquaculture has more than doubled.

Today, roughly one-quarter of all the seafood we eat comes from seafood farms. While most kinds of fish can only breed and grow in the wild, popular species like shrimp, salmon, catfish, carp, tilapia, and mussels can be grown using aquaculture. In the places where wealthy people shop, these farmed species (too expensive for most poor people to afford) are taking the place of more and more wild species.

You might think that for every fish and shrimp grown by aquaculture wild fish in the oceans are saved, but in many cases the opposite is true. To help them grow fast, farmed shrimp and carnivorous fish like salmon are fed fish-food made from wild ocean fish. While wild fish in the seas support marine ecosystems that provide food for all people, farmed shrimp and salmon usually end up on the plates of only wealthy people.

Small fish for sale at a street market in Indonesia.

Today

The Future?

Food for Thought

On a recent trip to the Raja Ampat Islands in eastern Indonesia, which may be the richest coral reefs in the world, scientists saw very few sharks. During the 500 hours they spent underwater looking for new species of fish and coral, scientists working for a conservation organization called The Nature Conservancy encountered only three large sharks. About 200 shark-finning boats fish around the Raja Ampat Islands, and scientists blamed the lack of sharks on overfishing.

Scavenger

Sharks as Recyclers

We think of them as predators, but many sharks are also scavengers. They clean the oceans of animal carcasses. At left, a blue shark feeds on a dead humpback whale.

A scientist touches the snout of a great white shark.

We Still Don't Know it All

Our knowledge about the roles sharks play in ocean ecosystems is limited. Sharks are difficult to keep in captivity and to observe for very long in the wild because many travel over huge areas. To learn more about the benefits sharks provide our oceans, the world needs young people to consider careers in shark biology and ecology. Some scientists are concerned that different types of sharks may become extinct before we have a chance to learn about their importance.

Predator

Keeping Populations Balanced

Sharks also help maintain a balance between different populations of their prey. Suppose one year the conditions are right and one particular species reproduces faster than another. Its population might eat all the food, leaving the other species to starve. Sharks and other predators help prevent this. If one type of fish reproduces like crazy in a particular year, sharks will hunt them like crazy because there will be a lot of them, and they'll be easier to catch.

A blue shark grabs a fish.

Ecosystem Balancer

A Shark's Job

One day while snorkeling where a reef's edge met deep water, Jackie and I saw a school of several hundred fusiliers, bright yellow and blue fish that eat plankton. Darting and swirling this way and that, the fusiliers moved together like dancers in a music video. Not a fish fell out of step as the school swam about in search of a meal.

Then I noticed one fusilier was having trouble swimming. I pointed it out to Jackie. It looked like part of its tail was missing. Suddenly, like a speeding car that surprises you when you're about to cross a street, a shark raced out of nowhere and grabbed the wounded fusilier. Gulp. In a bite it was gone.

Later, when our hearts stopped pounding, Jackie and I went to the aquarium to tell our friend, the marine biologist, what we'd seen. He smiled when we told him. Ever notice, he asked us, how people in a family sometimes look alike? Maybe you have your mom's eyes or your dad's long legs. These and other characteristics like hair color and height, he explained, are called **traits**, and you inherit your traits from your parents.

Fish do too. Some have their fathers' speedy shapes or are strong like their mothers. Unfortunately for fish, (and people too) there are traits that would be better not to inherit. Inheriting a shape that made you slower would be a bad trait to have if all the other fish in your school were fast.

This, we learned, is where sharks and other predators enter the picture. They go after weak and injured fish like that fusilier because they're easier prey. It may sound odd, but this actually does fish populations a favor. By eating the sick, slow, and stupid fish, sharks help ensure those fish don't spread diseases or reproduce and pass unfavorable traits on to the next generation. In this way sharks keep the populations of their prey strong and healthy. Maintaining the health of fish populations, of entire marine ecosystems, is part of the **niche** (or job) of sharks and other **apex predators** (predators at the top of the food web).

Shrinking Fish

As overfishing makes humans the sea's top predators, different traits are being passed on to new generations of fish. Unlike sharks, fishermen usually target the biggest fish in a population. This means that fish don't live as long, so heredity now favors fish that can start reproducing at a younger age. The effect is that overfishing is causing some fish species to become smaller.

They all look alike.

Food for Thought

Because we don't understand all the connections among the sea's creatures, overfishing can cause unexpected things to happen. In Tasmania, when people began fishing for sharks the number of lobsters they caught suddenly decreased. Later it was learned that with fewer sharks to prey on them, the local population of octopi had exploded. Guess what an octopus eats? Lobsters!

Female olive ridley sea turtles arrive on a Costa Rican beach to lay their eggs. All sea turtles once nested in numbers like this throughout the world.

Without Sharks?

Imagine an old Greek stone temple like the one on this page. Let's use it to represent an **ecosystem** (a community of living and non-living things). The columns hold up the roof and keep the building from collapsing, just as all living things support an ecosystem. Take out a column or two. Does the building fall? Probably not, but the burden of holding up the roof now rests more heavily on the remaining columns. This is what happens in an ecosystem when certain creatures become scarce or extinct. Sometimes other plants and animals are able to take over the niches of those that are missing. Sometimes they're not. The point is that as we remove more columns from a building, or species from an ecosystem, we come closer and closer to a collapse. What's left is a weaker, less complex community. This new ecosystem will be unable to support the same variety and abundance of life it once did.

What can History Teach Us?

In the 1500s, hundreds of millions of green sea turtles lived in the Caribbean Sea. When Christopher Columbus first sailed into the region, one of his crew thought it would be possible to walk to shore on the backs of sea turtles. Since then, green turtles have been hunted almost to extinction. Today, their Caribbean population has shrunk to just tens of thousands. Only now are scientists beginning to understand how the region's marine ecosystems were affected.

Lawnmowers

Here's how the system probably worked. Green sea turtles love sea grass, a type of grass that grows in shallow water, often close to shore. When Columbus arrived, enormous herds of greens and manatees (marine mammals which have also been hunted to near extinction) grazed vast sea grass meadows and actually kept them healthy. Like lawnmowers, they never let the sea grass grow very long. Today, however, there aren't enough green sea turtles or manatees to clip the sea grass, and it grows so long that it falls over on itself and rots. In many places throughout the Caribbean, sea grass meadows have become diseased and died.

Biodiversity

Like dominoes falling, the collapse of turtle populations and sea grass habitats has reduced the numbers of other creatures. Baby reef fish, shrimp and shellfish hide in sea grass. These creatures are food for stingrays, octopi and flounders that are prey for lemon sharks and other predators that count on finding a meal over sea grass meadows. This tiny snapshot shows how the lives of creatures are connected. Ecosystems thrive on the connections created by an enormous variety and abundance of life.

Today we are just beginning to realize how certain species (like green turtles and sea grass), keep entire marine ecosystems healthy. Scientists call these important plants and animals **keystone species**. Ten or twenty years from now, what might we discover is the result of our appetite for sharkfin soup?

A green sea turtle grazes on sea grass.

Food for Thought

The Caribbean monk seals pictured on the fallen column in the stone temple are **biologically extinct**. There are no more left. Plants and animals can also be **ecologically extinct**. This means they have become so rare that they can't interact with other members of their ecosystem in a meaningful way. In other words, a few are still around, but they do little to help hold up the building. The green sea turtle is a species that some people think is ecologically extinct because there are no longer enough to maintain the health of the sea grasses.

Extinction

45

Good Luck Soup

Facai, or black moss, is a plant that lives in dry sandy regions of Northwest China. Also known as "fat choy," facai looks like human hair and grows twisted throughout the roots of other plants. Unfortunately, collecting facai is destructive. As much as 16,000 sq/meters of grassland, an area bigger than five Olympic-sized swimming pools, is stripped bare to get just a few hundred grams of facai. Because facai collecting is turning thousands of square kilometers of grassland into desert, the Chinese government recently banned its sale, but the law has not been enforced.

Bird's Nest Soup

The dried spit of tiny Southeast Asian birds is the prized ingredient of this soup. On the walls of high caves male swiftlets make their nests entirely out of saliva. It comes out like wet noodles, but as it dries, it hardens like glue. Nests without a lot of feathers, sticks and dirt in them, sell for as much as US$2,000/kilo. Like sharkfin soup, bird's nest soup is flavored with chicken broth and sometimes pork, mushrooms and eggs.

Scientists say swiftlet populations have declined 75% since the 1960s, and the birds are unlikely to survive the growing demand for their nests.

A storefront sign in Singapore.

Bird's Nest Soup Recipe

100 grams bird's nest (dried)

1.5 liters chicken stock

1 large chicken breast (deboned)

15 ml dry sherry

60 ml rich chicken stock

2 egg whites

5 ml salt

2 green onions (minced)

15 grams ham (minced)

30 ml cornstarch

"Since bird's nest tastes kind of bland, a good chicken stock made with Chinese ham is perfect for making bird's nest soup," said Stephanie Yuen, a Canadian food writer and television host.

Tiger Penis Soup

Laws are supposed to protect tigers all over the world, but the demand for their body parts in China, Taiwan, South Korea and other Asian nations is so great that they continue to be killed. The most desired tiger part is the male's penis. It's made into a soup that sells for more than US$300/bowl.

"Unless it is stopped," said Tariq Aziz, an Indian wildlife conservationist, "our tiger population will be wiped out in less than 10 years." India has the world's largest surviving population of tigers, perhaps 4,000, down from 50,000 in 1900.

The Spoon is Mightier Than the Sword

I remember the first green sea turtle Jackie and I ever saw. His long tail told me he was a male, and he let us swim right beside him. His shell was as large as a dining room table for six. You wouldn't think an animal so big could be so graceful, but underwater sea turtles seem to fly with the speed of birds.

Five hundred years ago, scientists estimate there were as many as 600 million green sea turtles in the Caribbean Sea. More turtles than wildebeests and zebras and antelopes roaming Africa's plains. More turtles than cars and motorbikes in Hong Kong, Taipei, Jakarta, Beijing, Shanghai, Tokyo, Seoul, Seattle and Los Angeles combined. Today, just thousands of green sea turtles swim in the Caribbean. What happened?

People killed them. Native Americans ate sea turtles, but it was the Europeans, and then the Americans, who turned killing sea turtles into a business. It was easy to do. Like salmon, sea turtles return to the same place they were born to lay their eggs. So, each year females were caught as they climbed up on the beaches of their birth to dig their nests. In the 16th-20th centuries, millions were butchered to become food for sailors, colonists, and Africans brought to the Caribbean to work as slaves.

A male green sea turtle.

Millions more were killed to make a soup for wealthy British and Americans. Centuries ago, green turtle soup became a prized and expensive dish. Its recipe can be found in English cookbooks from the 1700s. Fancy restaurants throughout America served it well into the 20th century, long after most of the Caribbean's turtle nesting colonies were nothing but empty beaches.

Is this so different from what's happening to sharks today? Learning about the Caribbean's green sea turtles showed me that overfishing is not a new problem. It seems to be part of human nature, no matter our heritage, to exceed the oceans' limits. Sharks and green sea turtles, I'm learning, aren't the only wild things we humans are gulping toward extinction. Other plants and animals are also in hot water.

Food for Thought

Why do shark fins, facai, swiftlet nests and tiger penises end up in soup? Tradition? Vanity? Health? Being able to buy sharkfin soup is said to show you're wealthy. Facai sounds like "to get rich" in Putonghua and Cantonese, two languages spoken in China, and eating it is supposed to bring good luck. Swiftlet nests are believed to have vitamins and proteins that keep women's skin smooth and prevent aging. Soup made from tiger penises is said to make men better husbands.

Human Nature

Affluence,

In the pictures above and below, small fish are all that's for sale at these markets in Bali, Indonesia.

When I learned that it's mostly affluent people who are eating the world's sharks, or at least their fins, it made me wonder: "Who eats most of the other seafood the oceans provide for free? Is it shared equally? Do rich and poor have the same opportunities to benefit from the ocean's extraordinary resources?" As time passed, these questions about **equity** or fairness, became ones I wanted to answer. In my heart I knew I didn't want to be a part of something if it wasn't fair.

First, I needed to know if I'm rich or poor compared to most people. Looking around my neighborhood it was hard to tell. Other families owned bigger houses and newer cars. Still, I already had a sense I was lucky. I had driven through many neighborhoods in my city where I saw people crowded into tiny houses. They didn't own cars. Instead they walked, rode a bike, or took a bus wherever they went. Their clothes weren't as new as mine, and the kids from these neighborhoods didn't go to my school. No question about it. I was fortunate.

Later, I visited a website belonging to The World Bank, an organization that collects information about the living conditions of people in nations throughout the world. In a report I found there called *Poverty Trends and Voices of the Poor*, I discovered how really privileged I am. As part of a school project I made this chart about affluence and poverty using information from the report.

NUMBER OF PEOPLE IN THE WORLD TODAY	6 BILLION
NUMBER OF PEOPLE IN POOR NATIONS WHO LIVE ON LESS THAN US $1/DAY	1.2 BILLION
NUMBER OF PEOPLE IN POOR NATIONS WHO LIVE ON LESS THAN US $2/DAY	2.8 BILLION
PERCENT OF THE POPULATION IN COUNTRIES OF EAST ASIA AND THE PACIFIC THAT LIVE ON LESS THAN US $2/DAY	49 PERCENT
—IN SOUTH ASIA	84 PERCENT
—IN LATIN AMERICA AND THE CARIBBEAN	36 PERCENT
—IN THE MIDDLE EAST AND NORTH AFRICA	22 PERCENT
—IN SUB-SAHARAN AFRICA	76 PERCENT

Women in Sulawesi, Indonesia sort a catch of small reef fish.

Less Than $2/day

Poverty & Equity

I couldn't believe it. Half the world's people have less money for food, clothes, a place to live, transportation, school and the doctor than I spend each day on lunch. Wow, compared to most people I am really rich, and my family's wealth gives me many choices that poor people don't have.

What does this have to do with sharkfin soup and sharing the ocean's resources fairly? Well, there are only so many fish in the sea. The number of sharks and other fish are **finite**. There's a limit to them. Anyone who has ever shared candy knows, if your brother gets more, you get less. Really, all I had to do is go to the places where poor people shop to see that most seafood feeds people who live on a lot more than $2/day.

Poorer people do not have as many choices about what to eat. As an individual, a human being, an affluent consumer, do I have any responsibility for poor people who depend on the sea as a source of food? I wondered if it was possible to make my eating habits line up with my **values**—with things that are important to me—like being considerate and fair. I wanted to try and understand the impacts of my eating habits, so I could make choices that didn't harm others.

Choices

Choices and quantities abound at this seafood market in the United States.

Food for Thought

"Greater equity in the oceans would contribute to reducing poverty and underdevelopment."
—The Ocean Our Future:
Report of The Independent
World Commission on the Oceans

Does Culture

Diners at a sharkfin restaurant in Singapore.

One day, my mom called me to watch a cooking show on television. Chefs were competing to see who could make better food. They had only one hour, and then three judges would taste everything and pick a winner. Normally, I'd snore through a program like this, but these two chefs, one from Hong Kong and the other from Japan, were making sharkfin dishes. I sat down on the couch.

Each chef had three assistants and they raced around the set of the show—two large kitchens—like teams of professional athletes. Sharp knives in the hands of one were a blur as he transformed mushrooms and vegetables into neat, little piles of ingredients. Another assistant made food leap and flip out of sizzling pans with just a twitch of his wrists. Beneath their watchful eyes, shiny pots sweated. Sometimes the camera showed us their contents boiling above the yellow-blue flames of the gas stoves. I was amazed as out of the cooks' choreographed chaos came creations as beautiful to look at as I imagined they tasted.

It was obvious that these chefs love to prepare and eat good food. Asians of all cultures are proud of their cuisine and cooking well is highly respected. Sharkfin soup is a dish with roots in Chinese culture, but its popularity has spread to other Asian cultures. Here I was watching a chef from Japan who could prepare sharkfin dishes well enough to compete against one of Hong Kong's best. Even though it made me hungry, and I admired the skill of the chefs, I had mixed feelings watching the show.

I often hear that cooking and eating sharkfin is "cultural," but what does that mean? What is culture? Does culture ever change? Is culture always correct? I found my dictionary. It listed eight meanings of culture. I read them all. The one that best fit said culture is "the beliefs, behaviors, habits, skills, art, institutions, etc. of a given people in a given period." Hmm, that wasn't so hard to understand. According to this definition, cooking is

Food is Culture

This whitetip reef shark was finned in Similan Island National Park in Thailand.

ever Change?

certainly part of culture. The whole point of the TV program was to show how chefs could make food that celebrated the "beliefs, behaviors, habits, skills," and "art" of their communities.

But, are cultures always correct? I thought about some beliefs, behaviors and habits of our ancestors that we no longer think are right. Things like slavery, racism, religious persecution, child labor, and a lack of rights for women came to mind. Once these were practices of many cultures, but today the vast majority of people think these beliefs and behaviors are wrong. It seems to me that culture is not always right. It can and does change, often in ways that cause people to act in more kind, considerate and responsible ways. Certainly the lives of millions of children and less fortunate people have been improved by changes in attitudes toward slavery, racism and other cruel cultural practices of the past.

I wondered if one day we would realize we've been foolish to kill so many sharks. I wondered about the consequences of overfishing, both for our oceans and for people who depend on the sea as a source of food.

One thing I do know. Limiting our consumption of sharks and ending overfishing will never become cultural practices unless more people learn about what our eating habits are doing to the oceans. Cultural attitudes about slavery, racism, child labor, religious persecution and women's rights didn't change by themselves. It took time, sacrifice and the courage of individuals, first to re-examine their own actions, and then to change their cultures' beliefs.

Chefs at work.

Food for Thought

Many Asians are careful not to waste food. Their countries are densely populated, and older people remember war times when food was scarce. While in western countries some people just eat a fish's filet and throw away the head, skin and bones, in many Asian cultures these are made into delicious foods.

A small squid fishing boat in Indonesia.

The Poor

For generations, millions of poor people living in small, coastal communities all over the world have relied on the oceans to provide them with the healthy diet essential for a happy life. For many, seafood is the only source of protein available. The right of the poor, to catch the fish they have always caught, should be respected and protected.

Future Generations

Children everywhere, like these boys on the island of Sumbawa, Indonesia, have a right to inherit oceans as full of life as those their parents and grandparents knew.

Consider Others

Consumers

Many affluent people feel that because they work hard, they have a right to spend their money as they please. To wealthy sharkfin soup consumers what matters most is taste, quality, price, and what eating certain foods says about their character. "You really can't have a banquet without sharkfin soup, or you will look cheap," said the head of Hong Kong's restaurant owners organization.

Commercial Fishermen

Commercial fishermen, fin dealers and restaurants are businesses. Businesses survive by making profits and that requires catching as many sharks as possible. After all, they're only doing what businesses do, providing consumers with a product they want: sharkfin soup. If they don't catch and fin as many sharks as they can, or offer their customers sharkfin soup, their competitors will. Commercial fishing and related businesses also provide jobs for many people.

Baby sharks at a market in Sabah, Malaysia.

Animals

A Buddhist monk at the shark conference called finning cruel. "When animals suffer what moral responsibilities do we have?" she asked. "Humans should have compassion for all creatures."

Rights in Conflict

In Taiwan I heard a fisherman say he had a "right" to fish for sharks. He owned his own boat, and like his father and grandfather, he caught sharks in nearby waters. He didn't fin sharks and dump their bodies overboard. Almost every part of the sharks he caught—teeth, skin, fins, flesh and skeletons—were turned into something people used.

My dictionary says laws and traditions give people **rights**—things we feel we're entitled to or deserve. Many people believe they have a right to catch and eat fish. But, what happens when the world's population grows so large that there aren't enough fish to go around and people's rights conflict? Do we all still have the same rights then, or can there be limits to people's rights? Do animals and ecosystems also have rights? How about the oceans? These questions puzzled me. To help myself better understand them, I made a list of different points of view.

Thinking about these opinions, I knew my sympathies had come to be with sharks, but there seemed to be something right in everyone's point of view. I wanted the Taiwanese fisherman to be able to fish. I believe what a monk I met at the shark conference in Taiwan said, that we have a responsibility to not make animals suffer pain. Neither should affluent people make life harder for the poor by catching the fish they have traditionally relied upon to feed their communities. I believe children should be able to know a world with sea life as plentiful as the one our ancestors inherited. It's my dream to dive with more sharks. I even have sympathy for affluent consumers and the chefs and commercial fishermen who serve them. They should be able to catch sharks and cook and eat sharkfin soup . . . but not so much that they put everyone and everything else's rights in jeopardy. The trick, I think, is recognizing *how much is enough?* We should let our understanding of the oceans' limits and our compassion for others guide our behavior toward the sea and its creatures.

Recognize Limits

Food for Thought

"This planet does not belong to the adults of today . . . . If the signatures of our children were needed to ratify decisions that effect their future, many of the destructive actions perpetrated today would certainly cease."

—Fredrico Mayor, Director-General of UNESCO (The United Nations Educational, Scientific and Cultural Organization).

Tourists

Each year thousands of divers pay millions of dollars to swim over coral reefs and photograph sharks and other sea creatures. Tourism also creates millions of jobs with airlines, hotels, restaurants, and taxi services.

A diver with a school of trevally (jacks) in Indonesia.

Are Governments

A blue shark.

Shark-Catching Countries	Finning Ban	Overfishing Prevention Plan
Australia	some	yes
Brazil	yes	no
Canada	yes	no
China	no	no
Costa Rica	yes	no
Ecuador	yes	no
European Union	being discussed	drafted
The Gambia	no	drafted
Japan	no	yes
India	no	no
Indonesia	no	no
Malaysia	no	no
Mexico	no	no
Oman, Sultanate of	yes	no
Philippines	no	no
Senegal	no	drafted
Spain	yes	no
South Africa	yes	drafted
South Korea	no	no
Taiwan*	no	no
Thailand	no	no
Vietnam	no	no
United States	yes	yes

*Some governments consider Taiwan a province of China.

Responsible Fishing

The Food and Agriculture Organization (FAO) is the part of the United Nations that works with countries to make fishing more responsible. Responsible fishing recognizes limits and ensures that the oceans will remain full of life. The FAO has written a list of suggestions meant to help nations teach their fishermen to be more responsible. The list is called the **Code of Conduct for Responsible Fisheries**.

The **International Plan of Action for Sharks** is another FAO list of fishing tips. It's goal is to help nations that fish for sharks and rays develop a plan for making sure their fishermen don't catch too many. It suggests that nations ban the finning and discarding of sharks, and it encourages countries to teach their fishermen how to collect information about the location, time, species, sex and the size of the sharks they catch. With this information governments can figure out whether, with each passing year, their fishermen are catching more or fewer sharks. The FAO also wants nations to protect the places where sharks breed and where their young find shelter.

Finning Bans and Conservation Plans

When this book went to press (February 2003), some nations had laws that totally banned (forbid) the finning of sharks in their waters. While finning bans are necessary, bans alone don't guarantee sharks protection. Laws don't deter all people. And if a nation's officials lack desire, money or workers, they may not enforce laws. Some of the bans listed in the chart at left may not be effective. The chart also tells you whether a country has a plan—as the FAO suggests—that requires fishermen to record their shark catches and ensures that there is no overfishing. Like finning bans, shark protection plans are not all created equal. Some are more effective than others.

Helping Sharks?

Late one afternoon by the beach my eyes traced the trail of sparkles the setting sun had left on the water on its way to the horizon. I wondered how many other people were watching the sun like me. Our planet's magnificent oceans touch the shores of nearly all the world's nations. We share them. They belong to you, to me, to everyone. Children of the future will inherit them from us as we did from our parents. Whether we're from Mexico, China, Indonesia, America, India, Europe, Australia, Korea, Japan, Kenya, Taiwan, South Africa, wherever—the sea connects us. To me this means we have a responsibility to one another and to the oceans to look out for them and ensure that populations of sharks and other sea creatures remain plentiful. The oceans give us this opportunity to work together to make the world a better place.

The United Nations, an organization that helps countries cooperate, is urging all fishing nations to stop killing sharks for only their fins and to stop catching sharks faster than they can reproduce.

Choices Matter

A boat called The Chien Chun fishes illegally for tuna off the west coast of Africa.

Crew members on a longliner fishing illegally wear masks to hide their identities.

Why isn't Government Action Enough?

Sadly, the advice of the United Nations is not being followed by most shark-fishing nations. Here are some reasons why.

Countries are **sovereign** (they rule themselves). Even though they belong to the United Nations, they don't have to do what it suggests.

Some fishermen ignore the rules. As long as there have been rules about fishing, following them has been voluntary. Even the wealthiest nations don't have enough patrol boats and port inspectors to check and see that everyone is following the rules. The lure of money is powerful, and on the open sea there is no one to make sure fishermen don't fin sharks.

Some countries lack money. It costs a lot to pay scientists to identify which sharks live off a nation's shores and to understand how many can be safely caught each year. Populations need to be constantly studied to prevent overfishing.

There is a huge market for fins. What message do wealthy people everywhere send fishermen when they say with their wallets that they are willing to pay US$100 or more for a bowl of sharkfin soup? Are they saying "stop finning," or "keep it up?"

Food for Thought

At least 125 nations are known to export shark fins to Hong Kong, China, the world's leading fin importer. Only a few nations have a plan to make sure their fishermen don't catch too many sharks.

Can't Wait

Tracking the Trade in Wild Animals and Plants

In November of 2002, whale sharks and basking sharks, the world's two largest fish, became the first sharks protected by an international treaty meant to prevent animals from being hunted to extinction. Each year, people make billions of (US) dollars catching wild animals, cutting and digging up wild plants, and selling them all over the world.

To prevent this international trade from threatening the survival of species, the governments of many nations have signed an agreement known as **CITES** (Sī-tees), which is the nickname for "The Convention on International Trade in Endangered Species of Wild Fauna and Flora." CITES gives governments a way to cooperate, so they can monitor, and if necessary, stop the trade of endangered species before it causes their extinction.

Listing the World's Endangered Species

The World Conservation Union or IUCN is an organization that works to educate people about extinction and about the benefits of restoring and protecting the ecosystems that preserve the planet's biodiversity. Its famous "**Red List**" is recognized as being an accurate list of plants and animals that are endangered. Besides whale and basking sharks, dozens of other sharks and rays are on the IUCN's Red List. Realizing a species is endangered is the first step, the IUCN believes, toward reducing threats to its survival. Species usually appear on the Red List before being listed by CITES.

Informing Others

Ask Before You Buy

These two pocket-sized cards, published by the Monterey Bay Aquarium (in California) and The Audubon Society (a US conservation organization), are meant to help consumers identify species of fish caught in ways that don't harm our oceans.

MONTEREY BAY AQUARIUM

Seafood WATCH

YELLOWFIN TUNA

West Coast Seafood Guide

Good until Spring 2003

BEST CHOICES

Abalone (farmed)
Catfish (U.S. farmed)
Caviar (farmed)
Clams (farmed)
Crab, Dungeness
Halibut (Pacific)
Lobster, Rock (CA, Australia)
Mussels (farmed)
Oysters (farmed)
Sablefish/Black Cod (AK, BC)
Salmon (CA, AK; wild-caught)
Salmon, canned
Sand Dabs
Sardines
Sea Bass, White
Shrimp/Prawns (trap-caught)
Squid (CA market squid)
Striped Bass (farmed)
Sturgeon (farmed)
Tilapia (farmed)
Trout, Rainbow (farmed)
Tuna, Albacore/Yellowfin/
Bigeye (troll/pole-caught)

PROCEED WITH CAUTION

Clams (wild-caught)
Cod, Pacific
Crab, Imitation/Surimi
Crab, King (AK)
Crab, Snow
Lobster, American
Mahi-Mahi
Mussels (wild-caught)
Oysters (wild-caught)
Pollock
Sablefish/Black Cod (CA,WA,OR)
Salmon (OR, WA; wild-caught)
Scallops, Bay/Sea
Shark, Thresher (U.S. West Coast)
Shrimp (U.S. farmed or wild-caught)
Sole, English/Petrale/Dover
Swordfish (U.S. West Coast)
Tuna, Albacore/Yellowfin/Bigeye
(longline or purse seine-caught)
Tuna, canned

AVOID

Caviar, Beluga/Osetra/Sevruga
Chilean Sea Bass
Cod, Atlantic/Icelandic
Crab, King (imported)
Lingcod
Monkfish
Orange Roughy
Rockfish/Rock Cod/Pacific Snapper
Salmon (farmed/Atlantic)
Sharks (except U.S. West Coast)
Thresher
Shrimp (imported)
Sturgeon (wild-caught)
Swordfish (Atlantic)
Tuna, Bluefin

AK = Alaska
BC = British Columbia
CA = California
OR = Oregon
U.S. = United States
WA = Washington

Choices for Healthy Oceans

Do You Love Seafood?
So do we, but some of our favorite fish are in trouble. They're overfished, or caught or farmed in ways that harm the environment.

You Have the Power
The wise choices you make when you buy seafood can help us enjoy fish now and forever.

How to Use This Guide
Carry this convenient seafood guide to restaurants and grocery stores. Check the green, red and yellow lists before you buy.

THE AUDUBON/
PACIFIC WHALE FOUNDATION

Special Edition
Seafood Wallet Card

Your choices can help make our oceans healthy again

Consumer demand has driven some fish populations to their lowest levels ever. But you can be part of the solution. You can choose seafoods from healthy, thriving fisheries.

Which fish you buy at the market and off the menu will determine the future of our oceans. You have the power to protect our marine life.

Carry this card in your wallet.
Unroll it when you go to restaurants or grocery stores with fish on your mind.

Recognizing that people everywhere love seafood but also want to take care of the oceans, the Marine Stewardship Council (MSC) is helping consumers make ocean-friendly seafood choices. They do this by putting their label on seafood caught sustainably by fishermen working to minimize destructive fishing practices and bycatch. The label benefits responsible fishermen by helping consumers identify seafood that was caught with care. By choosing environmentally friendly seafood, the MSC believes consumers can make sure the world's supply of seafood lasts for the future.

Responsible Predators

I remember when my little brother first learned the word "predator." My dad was reading us a book about dinosaurs. "Tyrannosaurus rex," it said, "was the fiercest predator to ever stalk the earth." For months my brother became the fiercest predator to ever stalk our house. He stomped, growled and chomped on all the furniture. It was hard not to laugh, especially when he said: "I am da wo-wolds fee-wist pwedator."

Now, I realize my brother was right. Me, you, all of us humans are apex predators. We may not look fierce, but today there are so many of us that the human consumer is the last link in just about every ocean food web. But, unlike Mr. Apex, T. rex, we don't have to eat any old or sick Triceratops we find. We can choose what we eat.

I no longer want my choices to support overfishing. I want to eat in ways that consider the future of animals, ecosystems, less fortunate people and tomorrow's children. I want my choices to support fishing that's **sustainable** and equitable (fair). **Sustainable fishing** is fishing that doesn't catch so many fish that a species can't maintain its own naturally abundant populations. It's also fishing that doesn't damage ecosystems or kill a lot of other sea creatures as bycatch.

Choosing seafood from only sustainable fisheries is not easy. Sometimes it can even bother other people if they don't understand why you're not eating something you used to enjoy. Explain yourself. No one truly wants to eat in ways that harm the oceans or take food away from the poor. On the opposite page are some of the many organizations trying to help consumers understand the impacts of their seafood choices.

Taking Action

Food for Thought

"Health is the capacity of the land (and the sea) for self-renewal. Conservation is our effort to understand and preserve this capacity."
—Aldo Leopold, A Sand County Almanac

Because it's been listed by CITES, nations whose fishermen hunt and export the fins of basking sharks, like this one off the coast of California, will now have to keep detailed records about how many they catch and sell. CITES also requires buying nations to keep records of the basking and whale shark fins, meat and other body parts that they import.

Tony Leung

"It's so cruel to just cut off their fins and dump them back into the ocean. I need to educate young people to show how we get these sharks' fins and let them make the choice of whether they still want to have sharkfin or not."

Tony Leung is a movie actor from Hong Kong.

Bobby Chen Sheng

"If we continue to consume shark products at our present rate, many species of sharks will become extinct in less than a lifetime. Only you have the power to preserve sharks and keep our oceans healthy. Make the right choice for your future. Please say no to sharkfin soup."

Musician Bobby Chen Sheng is from Taiwan

Rodney Fox

"After my shark attack, I wanted to go back into the wonderful underwater world, but I was very frightened. I wanted to find out as much as I could about my attacker and other shark species. The more I learned, the less frightened I became. Now I think all sharks are great. We have to learn to live with sharks and keep a sustainable number in our oceans."

In 1963, Australian Rodney Fox was attacked by a great white shark. Since then he has devoted his life to learning about and protecting sharks.

Merry Camhi

"From the time I was a teenager, I knew that I wanted to help the world's animals, so I became a biologist. Right now I am working to protect sharks from overfishing. Most sharks grow slowly, mature late, and produce few young, so they can't keep up with the fishing pressure. There's still a lot more we don't know. How about becoming a scientist so that you can help discover more about sharks and work to ensure that they don't disappear from our oceans?"

Dr. Merry Camhi works for the National Audubon Society.

Heroes...

Zoe Tay

"We know that the shark is a superb swimming machine and that its powerful fins play a great part in its seemingly effortless glide through the depths of the oceans. Sadly, however, sharks are butchered because of their magnificent fins."

Like Chen Hsing-Yu, daughter of Taiwanese president Chen Shui-bian, Singaporean actress Zoe Tay recently broke with tradition and did not serve sharkfin soup at her wedding.

Tony Wu

"I spend a lot of time underwater, and one of my favorite experiences is seeing and photographing sharks in their natural habitat. Sadly, I'm coming across fewer and fewer sharks now, because so many have been hunted for their fins. Help me to ensure that these magnificent fish continue to grace the oceans, rather than our soup bowls."

Underwater photographer, writer and conservationist Tony Wu lives in Singapore.

Ang Lee

"Indulging in expensive dishes such as sharkfin soup, sturgeon, Napoleon wrasse and bear paw soup has become a growing trend. Most of the wild animals in high demand are rare or endangered. Illegal poaching has reached astronomical levels to satisfy this growing consumer demand, and many species are pushed to the brink of extinction. So, next time you are about to enjoy an exotic meal, please, be aware that your chopsticks could become a big threat to the survival of wild animals."

Taiwanese movie director Ang Lee's films include "Crouching Tiger, Hidden Dragon."

Singapore Airlines and Thai Airways recently decided to stop serving sharkfin soup to their first and business-class passengers. Why would these companies, in business to serve people, do something that might be unpopular? Because customers with different opinions spoke up. They wrote letters and asked the airlines to stop supporting finning by serving sharkfin soup on their flights. The airlines listened.

Food for Thought

Snorkeling with manta rays.

The two celaphalic fins that stick out in front of a manta's face deflect plankton into its mouth.

Big mantas can weigh 1,500 kilos and measure 5 meters or more from wingtip to wingtip.

Spread...

On a day so calm we could see the clouds' reflections on the ocean's surface, Jackie and I returned to the reef where I saw my first shark. We were pulling on our flippers at the water's edge when Jackie noticed them. "Look," she yelled, pointing out over the reef. I followed her gaze and there, a hundred meters out, I saw them—about a half a dozen black fins all bunched together. They seemed to be circling. As one or two broke the surface, others slid silently out of sight. We watched, frozen by the wonder they welled up inside us.

"What are those?" I gasped, as a lump squeezed down my throat and dropped into my stomach. Without a closer look, there was no way to tell, so together Jackie and I jumped off the rocks and headed straight for the fins. I dove down a bit and looked as far ahead as I could. We were swimming out into deep water. I could see the reef below, but the view before us was hazy.

And then we saw them . . . manta rays, giant relatives of sharks. Winged beings with specialized fins that stick out in front of their mouths like the horns some people draw on the heads of imaginary devils and demons. Years ago their appearance caused many people to fear them, but today we know mantas are gentle, and those fins on their heads? They help steer food into mantas' mouths.

It was impossible not to feel astonished by the mantas now swimming all around us. We counted as many as eight, but it was hard to keep track as they swooped, looped the loop, and spiraled upward to cruise with just their wing tips above the surface.

Continued on page 63

Food for Thought

"Unless someone like you cares a whole awful lot, nothing is going to get better. It's not."
—from The Lorax by Dr. Seuss

"Look in to my eyes."

The Future

the WORD!

Continued from page 61

The water around us was cool and full of plankton. A strong current was bringing this living soup up to the surface. Like whale sharks and basking sharks, mantas are filter feeders and this concentration of plankton had become their feast. Without realizing it, Jackie and I had swum into the middle of the mantas' meal. Several were flying right toward us. For a moment we thought these enormous fish would crash into us, but they always pulled up or veered to one side or another, often passing less than an arm's length away. They knew exactly where we were. Some even seemed interested in Jackie and me and swam right beside us, letting us stare into their big black eyes.

In the eyes of these mantas I saw some of my own feelings returned. Whenever I have a chance, I try to look into the eyes of the sea creatures I encounter. In sea turtles I've seen a look of peacefulness, in sea lions playfulness, in dolphins joy, and in an octopus I know, curiosity. My friends who've never experienced this think I'm crazy, yet they have no problem looking into the eyes of their cats and dogs and seeing a look of gratitude or happiness returned to them.

Thinking about what's happening to sharks and other sea creatures in our oceans, I've searched for a reason to believe things can change for the better. I have found one in myself. While governments have limited power to change people's behavior, when it comes to ourselves, we're powerful. Without shouting or writing letters, each one of us can help create a future for sharks and people. We just have to start by eating less sharkfin soup, or better yet, not eating it at all. Next, we need to do our best to explain our reasons for making this decision to our family and friends. If enough of us stop eating sharkfin soup, then fishermen won't catch so many sharks.

It would be a shame if sharks and other sea creatures became so scarce that we rarely encountered them, except on the end of a fork, in a spoon, or between two chopsticks. We don't want to give up the opportunity to look into the eyes of these magnificent animals. I suspect Jackie and I aren't the only ones who want to swim in seas full of mantas and sharks.

Food for Thought

"Never doubt that a small group of thoughtful, committed people can change the world; indeed, it is the only thing that ever has."
Margaret Mead, anthropologist

Joel Simonetti

Few things astonish me more than the life I discover underwater. As boys, my brother and I spent hours snorkeling and fishing in a lake near our home. Late at night we used to net minnows. My dad and I would hold the net across the mouth of a small stream, and my brother would splash down the creek scaring fish our way. Before we could see them, we could feel the fish knocking into the net. It was so exciting. "What would we catch this night?" When we raised the net in the moonlight, the fish bounced around like shiny, new coins skittering across a table. Bullheads, bass, chubs, daces, shiners, sawbellies and sticklebacks—we learned the names of the dozens of different kinds of fish we caught. Out of all these, we only kept a few of the sawbellies, which we used as bait the next morning to catch trout. I spent my early years like this—chasing and admiring fish. I don't think I've changed much, except these days I'd rather just snorkel and dive with big fish instead of catch and eat them. I hope my children and kids everywhere have the same chances I've had to be amazed by what awaits their discovery in our oceans, lakes and streams.

Lisa Cook

I will never forget how I felt the first time I saw the ocean. I was 10 or 11 and my father had planned a trip to see a herd of famous, wild ponies on a small island off the east coast of the United States. My dad and I were crazy about horses; we spent a lot of our free time riding together in the woods joel fields near our home. But it was not those ponies that would capture my attention or my heart. It was the crashing waves and the driving wind that pelted my legs with sand. It was the smell and the taste of the air that I fell in love with on that island.

We all know where we belong, whether we were raised there or not. We know. Some people belong in the mountains. They only feel really alive where the air is crisp and the trees are thick. Others belong in the desert. They delight in the dry heat, the midnight bloom of a cactus and the howl of a coyote. And then there are those of us who need to swim with sharks.

About the Authors

Index